Services in the Mobilization
for Youth Experience

EDITED BY HAROLD H. WEISSMAN

ASSOCIATION PRESS   NEW YORK

INDIVIDUAL AND GROUP SERVICES
IN THE MOBILIZATION FOR YOUTH EXPERIENCE

Copyright © 1969 by
National Board of Young Men's Christian Associations

Association Press, 291 Broadway, New York, N. Y. 10007

SBN: Hardbound edition 8096-1724-2
Paperback edition   8096-1731-5

Library of Congress catalog card number: 69-18843

PRINTED IN THE UNITED STATES OF AMERICA

Education

TO
WINSLOW CARLTON
Chairman of the Board
Mobilization For Youth

For Dedication and Devotion
to the Objectives of
the Program

Preface

At its founding, there were several program aspects which distinguished Mobilization For Youth from other social agencies. One was that Mobilization allocated a sizable portion of its resources to research. Yet even with these substantial resources, research could not concern itself with all of the agency's programs. Decisions as to priorities were based on the projected effectiveness of various programs, their relation to the theory which provided the foundation for the overall project, and whether the programs could conform to the rigors of research methodology without compromising either their quality or purpose.

Some programs were researched in great detail, others only in relation to specific aspects, and some unfortunately had to be left uninvestigated.[1] By early 1965, it was clear that much of the experience of the agency would be lost unless it was systematically described and analyzed.

Of particular concern was the practice knowledge that had been gained—the reservoir of insights, ideas, experiences, and judgments about the range of interaction and interventions staff were involved in, the structures and mechanisms they had devised, and the results achieved through their efforts.

To codify and refine this practice knowledge, MFY applied for a grant from the Office of Juvenile Delinquency and Youth Development of the Department of Health, Education and Welfare. Grant No. 67224, effective July 1, 1966, through June 30, 1968, provided for a Program Reporting Department consisting of a

---

[1] A list of the research studies and reports about Mobilization programs is appended to Vol. 4, *Justice and the Law*, as well as an epilogue and a discussion of the administration of the total MFY program.

staff of writers and program analysts. According to the grant's stipulations, the department was to

> . . . tell the story of each program division from its beginning, inserting at the appropriate places changes or new emphases divergent from those originally conceived, problems which emerged during the course of the program and how they were dealt with, techniques and methods which were used successfully and unsuccessfully, involvement with other MFY programs, participation statistics as well as any other pertinent statistical information. It will also include descriptions of program accomplishments, and other useful information relating to aspects of the program such as training and hiring of staff, administration and supervision. The intention . . . is to provide people who have participated in a unique social adventure with an opportunity to develop their own ideas and practice insights and to exchange them with others similarly engaged.

A few of the papers which appear in this book and the other volumes in this collection were written by line staff members of the particular divisions; most were written by the Program Reporting staff; some are an amalgam of the work of both line staff and Program Reporting staff. A member of the Program Reporting staff was assigned responsibility for the reports on each of the program divisions of Mobilization. This responsibility included gathering all prior reports and published material of the division, developing with line staff an outline for the projected volume, observing the operation of programs, preparing working drafts—alone or in conjunction with line staff—and discussing these with all staff involved with the topic being covered.

All the papers in this volume went through several drafts; many were substantially altered, some were combined, and some, after discussion with the staff, were deleted. In addition, former executives of the agency—particularly Dr. Richard Cloward, director of research, and Dr. Charles Grosser, formerly assistant director of action programs—gave their comments and suggestions. Their help was invaluable in ensuring the accuracy and quality of the material presented.

As editor of this volume, it was my responsibility to make final decisions as to what material should be included, what should be emphasized, what value should be accorded various conflicting ideas and sentiments, and what conclusions should be drawn. In this process it was necessary for me to rework many of the papers in the interest of economy of time and effort. If the results are valuable, a major share of the credit must go to Hettie Jones, who took responsibility for the papers on Services to Individuals and Families, and to Beverly Luther, who performed the same function for the Group Services papers. They did the hardest part of the job.

There are a great many able people to whom considerable credit is due. Foremost is Bertram M. Beck, executive director of Mobilization since 1965; he first conceived the idea for these volumes and was instrumental in obtaining the grant that made them possible. Special note must be made of the time and effort which Group and Individual Services staffs gave to the preparation of this volume. It is not easy or comfortable to be observed and questioned for long periods of time. Margaret Shea, director of Services to Individuals and Families, and Sherman Barr, assistant director, were particularly helpful, as was Phillip Kramer, director of the Department of Group Services.

Danielle Spellman, Nancy Dannenberg, and Martha King typed and retyped the papers, not without complaint but always with humor and concern. Each of them also, when the need arose, assisted in observing programs and were helpful critics of the papers.

Beverly Luther served as my assistant in this project. Without her help it could not have been brought to a conclusion. She relieved me of a variety of administrative duties and faultlessly followed through with innumerable details. Gladys Topkis edited the papers, as she has done with so much of the written material produced at Mobilization. A considerable portion of the credit for the style and clarity of the material goes to her.

This book and each of the other three volumes—*Community Development, Employment and Educational Services, Justice and the Law*—begin with a statement of the ideas and concepts the workers intended to apply in a particular program division. The individual papers which make up each volume describe what happened when these ideas were put into effect and what was learned from the experience. Some of the papers deal with the history of a specific program, some deal with broad issues and concerns in social work and other professions, and others describe experiences in many programs. The concluding chapter in each section summarizes the major issues which emerged from the experiences described.

The four volumes are meant to constitute an intellectual history of a project which in all likelihood represents a watershed in the development of social welfare in America. This type of history perforce emphasizes learning. It does not tell the comprehensive history of the agency. It may even dwell more on failures than prudent public relations would dictate. The volumes, as such, are not intended to provide a balanced picture of the agency. They are intended, rather, to give readers an opportunity to share the insights, ideas, experiences, and judgments of those who shaped and were shaped by it.

—H. H. W.

Contents

Introduction

The slum is, in its least complex form, a disorderly mechanism for human destruction, operating through crumbling houses and relatively unconnected inhabitants in a loosely defined geographic area. At its most developed, it is a homeland for a particular minority group or assemblage of groups, a neighborhood with its own traditions, where a foreign language may be the common tongue and where the accepted customs, loyalties, and hostilities may be divergent from, or even directly opposed to, those of society outside. New York City encompasses a wide assortment of slums, of all sizes and conditions, in all stages of development and disorder. Among them, Manhattan's Lower East Side has the longest history as a slum neighborhood, although the component languages and customs have changed several times through the years and are not uniform today from one group's heartland in the area to another's.

The Lower East Side first became a slum neighborhood thanks very largely to the Irish Potato Famine of 1846, which drove the impoverished "wild geese" abroad as mercenaries and refugees. Irish immigrants began to pour into America in the 1840's and 1850's. New York received a larger number than any other city, and several parts of the Lower East Side became Irish homelands, especially the Five Points area, where a small Irish enclave still exists, and the area along the East River, where many Irish were employed on the docks. The zone near the Bowery became a drinking and red-light district. Like later minority groups who felt themselves isolated by poverty in the middle of the New Paradise they had come to find, the Irish formed gangs. The famous Bowery Gangs included both adults and adolescents, and controlled their "turf" with savagery. And, as was true of later delinquent and gangster groups, the Irish proved to be useful to the powers-that-be—in this case Tammany Hall—who found employment for the Irish Bowery Gangs during elections and a value in the Irish vote.

Then the Irish took over Tammany Hall and became American, through the acquisition of political power and the process of acculturation. They were fortunate in that this process for them did not involve learning a foreign language or accepting a basically alien culture. In the eyes of some of the groups that succeeded them on the Lower East Side, the image of the American was that of the Irishman.

The Germans began arriving in the 1860's and 1870's and became for a time the most numerous immigrant group in the city. In the 1860's it was estimated that two thirds of the 120,000 German-born residents of New York City lived on the Lower East Side in an area which the immigrants called *Kleindeutschland,* or *Deutschlandle.* Many of the Irish moved away, and the beer halls and delicatessens of Germany were duplicated on the streets of the Lower East Side.

This German Lower East Side seems to have been a comparatively peaceful slum. Many of the immigrants were artisans. There were fewer peasants than among the Irish, and big city living, in their recreated Germany, seems to have come fairly easily to them. The Germans, even given the handicap of their foreign language, were a group whose customs, tastes, and personal appearance did not militate against their relatively undramatic integration into American society.

This was not the case with the next two immigrant groups to arrive in the Lower East Side. The eastern European Jews and the primarily southern Italians who came in hordes toward the end of the nineteenth century were foreign in their customs, looks, and language, with a tendency to shout and laugh in public too loudly for the taste of traditional America, surrounded with the aura of sensuality and depravity with which lighter-skinned races have always tended to endow those darker than themselves.

The center of Little Italy lay west of the Lower East Side, but the Italian population extended well into the area. The immigrants were almost all peasants or else refugees from the hideous slums of Naples and Palermo and Agrigento. They came to America in swaying ships packed with hundreds of their fellows, and were met by waiting relatives who took them to the tenements that would be their new homes. The tubs of family washing and the piles of sewing to be done on a piecework basis might already be prepared for the girl, the address of the gang-labor contractor and his assurances of "plenty of work for a boy from the old hometown" welcomed the man. They constructed their Little Italy as well as they could, but for a Sicilian peasant, the sidewalks of New York buried in snow differed in more than geography and climate from the sun-baked, rocky farmlands of Sicily. The southern Italian came from a region of feudal landlords who were still called barons, an intensely traditional and immovable society; in America everything seemed in flux and up for grabs, provided that one was ruthless or knowledgeable enough. Those who were not struggled along; those who were rose out of areas like the Lower East Side into the goods and benefits of middle-class American living, through the routes of business, politics, dogged and desperate acquisition of a professional education, or crime. For some there was a bitter price to be paid in renunciation, in self-hatred for the foreignness which the parents had given and the child still, in spite of himself, retained. American acceptability often came at a profound psychological cost.

The eastern European Jews were the group that most characterized the Lower East Side in the first half of the twentieth century. In New York, in the nation at large, and outside America, the Lower East Side came to mean the Jewish ghetto. By 1900, the East Side was already the largest, most densely populated Jewish community in the world. Of two million Jewish immigrants in America at the time of World War I, three quarters had lived for a time on the Lower East Side. Although there remained scattered pockets of other ethnic groups—Italians, a handful of Germans, small neighborhoods of Irish, an enclave of Slavonic people—virtually all of the Lower East Side, from Cherry Street to Tenth Street, from the East River to the Bowery, was considered the ghetto.

The Russian pogroms of the 1880's and 1890's were the propelling force for the Jewish immigration. There had been a settlement of German Jews on the Lower East Side before then, and these now Americanized Germans tended to be ill at ease with their alien coreligionists, condescending and superior. Some of them owned the garment businesses in which the new arrivals were employed. Other German Jews were active in philanthropy and in attempts to Americanize the immigrants.

The East European Jews themselves were divided into groups who spoke different dialects of Yiddish and had somewhat different customs. Russians, Lithuanians, Poles, Galicians, and Romanians tended to settle among their own and preserve their own cultural variants, but they could easily understand each other's Yiddish. The Lower East Side became a center of Yiddish culture, with a developed literature, an extremely active theater, and six flourishing newspapers, including the still existing *Daily Forward*. In its time, the *Forward* was an important Socialist newspaper, in the forefront of the Jewish labor movement during the days of the early unions and the violent strikes.

The Jewish East Side has become known, through the writings of nostalgic former residents, as a foreign enclave, with foods and sounds and colors and customs that marked it apart from the larger society. It was that, of course, but it was also a tenement slum where the measure of success was departure, where the young members of street gangs fought and developed into full-time hoodlums struggling with the Irish and Italian gangsters for the vast spoils of Prohibition.

America's first settlement house, the University Settlement, was founded on the Lower East Side in the 1880's. The settlement movement on the Lower East Side pioneered in attempts to deal with the problems of slums, such as campaigns for increased recreational facilities, housing reform, and child-labor legislation.

In the 1930's and 1940's the ghetto began to break up. Many Jews moved to the Bronx and Brooklyn, leaving behind the old, the economically trapped, and the failures. In the next two decades another group of immigrants arrived to change once again the complexion and language of the Lower East Side. Puerto Ricans have come in vast numbers from the slums of Ponce and San Juan and New York's East Harlem, joined by lesser numbers of Negroes from the American South or from New York's Harlem or Bedford-Stuyvesant. The combined Negro and Puerto Rican population of New York City increased 250 percent between 1925 and 1950. A small colony of Puerto Rican cigarmarkers had lived on Cherry Street in the Lower East Side since the 1920's, but the major destination of the postwar Puerto Rican immigration to New York City was "El Barrio," East Harlem centering around Third Avenue and 101st Street. The Negroes coming up from the South and the West Indies went first to Harlem and later to Bedford-Stuyvesant, which were long-established Negro ghettos. Therefore, for the Puerto Ricans and Negroes who began moving down to the Lower East Side in the 1940's and 1950's as the Jewish population vacated the tenements, the Lower East Side was not a primary area of settlement, a homeland, as it had been for the Germans and the Jews, but a spillover area without structure or traditions.

Many of the tenement streets awaiting the newcomers were little different from what they had been fifty or sixty years before, but the postwar building boom had swept some of the others away. Low-income public-housing projects and middle-income cooperatives have been built on the Lower East Side. The cooperatives have brought the middle class into the neighborhood for the first time in a century, to join the low-income Puerto Ricans and Negroes who live in the tenements and public-housing projects. The residents of the cooperatives are generally middle class or so-called stable working class whites, primarily Jewish. In the tenements east of Avenue B, the western boundary of the Mobilization For Youth project, almost none of the previous white residents remain. In recent years, increasing though still relatively small numbers of a different kind of slum dweller have arrived: artists and those who attach themselves to artistic communities, drawn by the low rents growing less and less available in Greenwich Village. In the parlance of renting agents, the Lower East Side is now the East Village, as a result of this movement and in the attempt to capitalize on it.

The section of the Lower East Side which Mobilization For Youth singled out as its target area is primarily a Puerto Rican slum. Some Italians still live in the southern portion, a small Slavonic group to the north, a number of Chinese on certain streets who are moving over from Chinatown to the west. Jews still own much of the housing and many of the businesses, and there are old-fashioned outdoor Jewish markets on Orchard Street and on Avenue C. From a survey of the Mobilization area taken in 1961, it was estimated that 27 percent of the population was Jewish, most of them residents of the cooperatives. But the basically Puerto Rican nature of the area is very evident from the record shops and bodegas and botanicas and the bongos out on the street at the first touch of spring.

The postwar wave of Puerto Rican immigration now seems to be nearing its end. The Puerto Ricans came, as citizens of the United States, for the economic opportunities which were wanting in Puerto Rico, and they stayed because, even in the rat-ridden tenements of El Barrio, things really were somewhat better here, or at least more promising.

New York offered many of the Puerto Ricans their first confrontation with direct racial prejudice. The pecking order of the oppressed tended to establish itself again as in America it usually, sadly has. A certain degree of hostility developed between Negroes and Puerto Ricans since they were competing for the same bottom-of-the-heap jobs and some of the same slum housing, and, less materially, because the bottom of society is a very narrow place for people to share. Recognizable Negro–Puerto Ricans, a minority among the immigrants, were in a very difficult position: On the one hand they had to deal with a double load of prejudice; on the other, many of them came to feel that being Spanish and black was somehow better than being simply an American Negro, and so they clung even more tenaciously to their language and denied all connection with the American black man. On occasion, as occurred in the process of rent-strike organizing activities on the Lower East Side, light-skinned Puerto Ricans have been told they were "more American" than the darker-skinned Hispanicos and used as a shock force against their own people.

Gradually that section of the Lower East Side which forms the Mobilization For Youth project area is becoming the kind of slum one can call a neighborhood. The Puerto Rican has come to feel at home in the Lower East Side, and the area has become a zone of "Spanish color." But even a slum that is a neighborhood continued to be a machine for human destruction. The difficulties with school that usually burden lower-class youngsters are multiplied for children whose native language is Spanish and whose cultural values are Caribbean. During the late 1950's, the "heroic era" of teenage gang warfare in New York City, some of the casualties took place on the Lower East Side where bopping gangs formed by kids of Puerto Rican, Italian, and Negro descent fought with adult weapons for control of their respective turfs. With the decline of the conflict gangs, and in part a reason for the decline, came a huge increase in heroin addiction throughout New York. The junkie on the nod as the result of a shot of horse became an everyday sight on the Lower East Side. And many of the junkies were adolescents, copping out young on the consumer's society that seemed to have very little in the way of possible consumption to offer them.

Along with the increase in addiction came an upsurge in petty theft. Slum dwellers are always the first to suffer from those among them who choose criminal activity. This pattern of declining gang conflict and rising heroin addiction and petty crime characterized juvenile delinquency on the Lower East Side when, in 1962, Mobilization For Youth actively undertook to "mount . . . a major demonstration program to attack the problem of juvenile delinquency" by "expanding opportunities for conventional behavior."

Mobilization For Youth had its inception at a meeting of the board of directors of the Henry Street Settlement in June 1957, where a report was read on the growth of delinquency on the Lower East Side. In the Mobilization area this rate grew from 28.7 offenses per 1,000 youths in 1951 to 62.8 per 1,000 in 1960. Appalled by the dimensions of the problem, the board proposed that research begin immediately on a program of massive response to the increasing rate of juvenile delinquency. A planning process began which took four and a half years to complete. During a preliminary stage, faculty members of the Columbia University School of Social Work, assisted by a grant from the Taconic Foundation, conducted research emphasizing the existing youth-serving agencies on the Lower East Side and what could be learned from them in terms of practice. In a second stage of research, beginning in November 1959 and made possible by grants from the National Institute of Mental Health, a unifying principle of expanding opportunities was worked out as a direct basis for action. This principle was drawn from the concepts outlined by sociologists Richard Cloward and Lloyd Ohlin in their book *Delinquency and Opportunity*. Drs. Cloward and Ohlin regarded delinquency as the result of the disparity perceived by low-income youths between their legitimate aspirations and the opportunities—social, economic, political, educational—made available to them by society. If the gap between opportunity and aspiration could be bridged, they believed delinquency would be reduced; that would be the agency's goal.

The geographical boundaries set for Mobilization coincided with the zone of greatest poverty and highest delinquency on the Lower East Side: Avenue B on the west, the East River on the east, East 14th Street to the north and the City Hall juction to the south running into a tip of Lower Manhattan. The area has a population in 1961 of approximately 107,000, of whom 27 percent were Jewish, 11 percent Italian, 25 percent other white, 8 percent Negro, 3 percent Oriental, and 26 percent Puerto Rican. These percentages do not reflect the ethnic groups served by Mobilization, however, for a considerable number of the whites, as we have noted, were financially stable, with little need for Mobilization services. The youth population was 90 per cent Puerto Rican and Negro. And the percentage of Puerto Rican and Negro residents almost doubled between 1960 and 1967.

More than half of the tenement housing (62.4 percent) was classified as substandard by the 1960 census. Although the city-wide unemployment rate in that year was 5.0 percent, some ninety neighborhoods (half of them in Manhattan) had rates at least twice the citywide figure. The Lower East Side contained one third of Manhattan's double-rate neighborhoods. Forty-one percent of its households received some form of financial assistance, and 37 percent of its adult residents had failed to complete the eighth grade.

A thirty-three-man board of directors was established for Mobilization, including eleven faculty members from the Columbia School of Social Work and leaders of various citywide and national agencies, such as the Office of the Commonwealth of Puerto Rico, the New York Community Service Society, and the Urban League. Major funding came from the City of New York, the National Institute of Mental Health, the Ford Foundation, and the President's Committee on Juvenile Delinquency.

Supplied with these resources and armed with its extensive background of preparation and research, Mobilization For Youth began its service projects in 1962, with an initial staff of approximately three hundred.

Besides a Division of Research, programs were grouped under four major divisions: Educational Services, Employment Services, Services to Individuals and Families, and Community Development. This latter division included Services to Groups. In 1964 a fifth division, Legal Services, was added.

The project from the first attracted much local and national attention because of the experimental nature of its programs and the prospect that, should Mobilization's modes of dealing with the problem of juvenile delinquency prove successful, similar programs might be mounted throughout the country. Many of the staff members were highly trained specialists; others were local residents who had had experience in community work; nearly all began their work with a high degree of commitment and enthusiasm. What follows is a record of their effort.

Henry Heifetz

Services to Individuals and Families

1

Overview of Services to Individuals and Families

Hettie Jones

There were poor people on the Lower East Side before 1962, perhaps even poorer than those who lived in the area when MFY
was launched. Many of them were able to make their way up and
out. How they did this and who helped them were important considerations to those who planned Mobilization's Services to Individuals and Families.

The history of efforts to deal with the problem of poverty in this
country can be traced as far back as the settlement of the land.

> *September 29, 1685.* The town this day by voat giveth ten pounds
> to John Bennet To be payd out of ye town treasury and to bee
> husbanded by leeftenant Nathanill Seely and Sargent Mathew Sher-
> wood about building a house and what else may be for that relief
> in thar afflicted condesion.

> *March 14, 1774.* Voted ye report of ye Com'tee appointed to con-
> sider of the best method to provide for the poor of the Town be
> accepted.[1]

It was to the "worthy poor" that the first volunteer "friendly
visitors" turned their attention. They and paid agents of charity
organizations, the counterpart of today's social workers, not only
determined whether or not a family qualified for financial aid but

[1] Fairfield, Connecticut, Town Records (minutes of town meetings), in
Ralph Pumphrey and Muriel Pumphrey, *The Heritage of American Social
Work* (New York, Columbia University Press, 1961), p. 23.

also attempted guidance and rehabilitation, stressing, of course, temperance and Christian virtue. Through most of the nineteenth century, a distinction was made between "honest poverty" and "pauperism which is willing to rely upon gifts and alms." The poor-and-worthy merited help; the unworthy must be cast out. However, a set of General Suggestions to Those Who Visit the Poor, published in 1879, included many points that have been retained in casework practice:

> Any notion of condescension or patronage is not only wrong in itself, but is also sure to do harm. . . . No eyes are keener of vision than those which have been sharpened by want.

> The visitor needs to cultivate the habit of looking below the surface of things, and not judging by first impressions.

> In every case the visitor should seek to foster a spirit of self-respect and independence.

> The poorest are those who have *no wholesome contacts with society or with each other*. . . .[2]

The worker, or visitor, was encouraged as well to become acquainted with all available medical and charitable facilities for the poor, with sanitary laws, and with "the nearest parks, squares, and other grounds open to people, and . . . the rules which govern their use." The worker was reminded that "the poor have legal rights which they often fail to enjoy," and that legal redress of wrongs "is one means of keeping the poor in wholesome sympathy with society, by making them feel that laws and courts are for rich and poor alike."[3] The poor were to be urged to be economical and to send their children to school, since public education was available.

In the latter part of the nineteenth century and the beginning of the twentieth, as social work itself became more organized and a body of knowledge was built up regarding social problems, social

[2] Rev. R. E. Thompson, *Manual for Visitors Among the Poor* (Philadelphia, J. B. Lippincott Co., 1879), pp. 14–21. Quoted in Pumphrey and Pumphrey, *op. cit.*, pp. 176–181.

[3] *Ibid.*

casework became more systematized as a method of helping people. As it was discovered that others as well as the poor could benefit from such assistance as casework could furnish, the ladies bountiful were replaced by social workers who had been to school (courses were instituted early in the twentieth century). The objects of their concern became "clients," persons whose character, physical condition or circumstances, or a combination of these, made them incapable of fully maintaining themselves in their social setting. What had been an art or perhaps a mission became an approach, involving such matters as diagnoses and professional relationships. With the acceptance of Freud's theories, caseworkers devoted much time to studying inner forces that had previously escaped their understanding of troubled people; during the 1920's this new psychology added much to what casework knew about human behavior.

But after the 1920's came the 1930's, and another perspective. The inner man was only part of a creature who could be shaped, battered, or smashed by social and economic forces quite beyond his control and often beyond his understanding. There were poor people again.

Until the 1930's, private social agencies had had to be concerned with the problem of providing financial relief as well as shoring up the souls or, later, the psyches of their clients. But with the establishment of government-financed public-assistance programs, caseworkers in private agencies came to spend all their time on the latter concern. Casework, except as it was practiced within public agencies, was now free to develop new methods of identifying and dealing with the complex problems of social existence that beset people in various economic categories. It seemed that private agencies were to deal with the emotional disorders of human beings, government agencies with their financial troubles. Those whose difficulties had mainly to do with their precarious or non-existent income thus became, of necessity, the clients of public agencies, and those whose difficulties could be considered more personal in nature sought the private agency. During the '40's and after the war, casework was still talking about the individual's psychosocial difficulties, the role network of the family, character disorders, interpersonal conflicts, personality disturbances, and casework-client relationships, and the "undermining effects of social stress upon adequate personalities."

There were not supposed to be poor people anymore. Public assistance had taken care of that. But suddenly, in the 1950's, the "other America" was rediscovered and contrasted angrily with the "affluent society." There were still poor people after all—people who needed help and services and who weren't getting very much of either—and they were busily producing the delinquents who fought on Henry Street in plain sight of its famous settlement house. Many were second-generation relief families. They kept away from the community centers, whose clientele was mainly those of the low-income group who were on their way up and out. And they kept away from private social agencies, where casework was becoming a careful science.

In an important and often quoted study of family agencies, Dorothy Fahs Beck found that the lower-income group was grossly underserved, even though its need was "obviously and historically greatest." [4] The poor of the 1950's seemed to require a kind of care different from that which was forthcoming; casework as practiced in the family agency was concerned with other people than they.

> The presenting problems of lower-class clients tend to be environ-
> mentally based and require immediate direct intervention; contacts
> with agencies are broken when this environmental intervention is
> not forthcoming. . . . Needs presented by lower-class clients require
> immediate service. . . . Estrangement, suspicion, ethnic differences,
> and language barriers also keep the lower-class client away from
> the private casework agency. . . . Poverty causes a multiplicity of
> problems in the slum family which the specialized services of the
> private agency are generally unable to cope with.[5]

[4] Dorothy Fahs Beck, *Patterns in the Use of Family Agency Service* (New York, Family Service Association of America, 1962). For a comprehensive discussion of this problem see Richard A. Cloward and Irwin Epstein, "Private Social Welfare's Disengagement from the Poor: The Case of Family Adjustment Agencies," in George Brager and Francis Purcell, editors, *Community Action Against Poverty* (New Haven, College and University Press, 1967).

[5] Charles Grosser, "The Nature and Theoretical Basis for the Program in the Mobilization For Youth Project," (mimeographed, New York, Mobilization For Youth, 1963).

Since they were not able to get the kind of help they wanted or needed from private agencies, poor people stayed away. The longer this estrangement continued, the greater became the distance between what was known about casework and what was known about poor people.

The professions, inevitably owned and operated by middle-class persons, have developed methodology which, in part, has failed to take into account the differing style and needs of low-income culture. Thus, although the verbal facility required of traditional psycho-therapeutic processes is ordinarily not found in lower-income social-ization, there are few attempts to develop treatment methods more relevant to these less verbal persons.[6]

This distance was implied in the very name assigned in the '50's to those whom social work no longer knew what to do about: the hard-to-reach. Although many agencies tried valiantly, they usually tried to reach what they termed the multi-problem family, and what they offered was a family-centered casework. But, as one observer noted wryly, "There often just ain't no families"—only kids and mothers and an occasional man.

Slowly new ideas about casework began to develop—notably in some of the Lower East Side agencies involved in the planning for Mobilization. There were in 1960 a considerable number of pri-vate agencies in the area, including five major settlement houses, some of which offered mental-health services. In addition there were public agencies such as the Board of Education, Welfare Department, the Youth Board, the City Department of Parks, the City Housing Authority, and the Lower East Side Neighborhoods Association.

Utilizing the resources of all these agencies as well as its own, Mobilization hoped to develop a new casework, the outlines of which were described as follows:

The question we must answer is: What types of person can be expected to be influenced in what ways by what types of program? The task is to make a differential diagnosis of the client's difficulties, to classify the differential influences which will be exerted by one

[6] *Ibid.*

or another program, and to bring the two together in a meaningful fashion. Such an approach—stressing the possibilities of altering behavior and personality through the imaginative reconstruction of social circumstances buttressed by appropriate supportive casework relationships—will, we believe, yield greater rewards in work with many low-income people.[7]

Preliminary research indicated that residents in the lowest-income group participated very little in any of the local agencies. MFY's target population—those who were the least served, those who participated least—needed to be brought to these available services, and the services in turn had to be reminded that some people were being left out. Within the broad objective of expanding opportunities, the program of Services to Individuals and Families (SIF) was designed to make people aware of existing opportunities and to induce them to use these facilities—in a sense, to overcome the self-defeating adaptations that prevented people from taking advantage of what was available to change their lives. The service that SIF was to provide was also an opportunity in itself, an experiment in giving the poor the help that did not appear to be forthcoming from other sources.

For a start, it was decided that at Mobilization there would be strong emphasis on concrete, immediate services—such as small loans of money, legal aid, escort service, and baby sitting—because the people of the MFY area suffer overwhelming social and economic problems which require service right then and there. It was deemed neither possible nor just to ask a person to "improve his circumstances through a better understanding of himself" (by means of an extended casework relationship which will begin at *next* week's appointment) when what is wrong at that particular moment is that he is out of work and has no money, and the baby needs milk. Whether these troubles stem wholly or in part from a person's lack of self-understanding was to be a matter for later consideration; the important thing was first to relieve the pressure of need. It was hoped that by changing the client's social circumstances, by reordering his environment sufficiently, a way might

[7] *A Proposal for Prevention and Control of Delinquency by Expanding Opportunities* (New York, Mobilization For Youth, 1961) p. 357.

be cleared for altering his pattern of response away from the self-defeating repetition, the trap of despair and hopelessness, the futility which appeared to pervade his life.

As part of this approach service was to be dispensed in an informal manner, through a decentralized system that would be conspicuously unlike the large, impersonal bureaucracies—public-assistance agencies, city hospitals—which low-income people are forced to confront. MFY also recognized the need to maximize its congeniality to those whom it intended to serve, which of course included approaching people with some idea and appreciation of their existence. It became necessary, therefore, for workers in the Services to Individuals and Families program to *know* how low-income people—specifically those of the Lower East Side—thought, felt, and acted.

It was planned that the SIF program would have a number of units, more or less distinct from one another but under the same administration and with a certain amount of interaction or intercommunication. Four neighborhood service centers were to be the main focus of the SIF program, offering a variety of under-one-roof services—a social caseworker, public-health nurse, visiting homemaker, escorts, and baby-sitters; a liaison-resources service composed of representatives of various municipal departments (Housing, Welfare, Health, etc.)—and an inquiry service which was to provide immediate, practical information on housing, education, welfare, legal, and consumer problems, and the like. The centers were also to provide training for students of social work and other helping professions.

A referral service operating out of the neighborhood service centers was to direct those in need of treatment to one of two local mental-hygiene clinics—University Settlement and Henry Street—each of which was to set up a unit under SIF administration. A social-planning service was intended initially to work with a limited number of especially troubled families and ultimately to integrate the various services available within the center. An experimental program for the reintegration of juvenile offenders was to be conducted by specially trained probation officers, taking advantage of other opportunities available within the program—Job Corps and Neighborhood Youth Corps, for example.

As will be noted in the papers in this section, several of the proposed programs were never started. Others changed dramatically over the years.

The new casework did not materialize in the form originally intended, yet the old casework roles of counselor and referral sources changed dramatically. Ideas about the proper and professional relationship among social agencies and their staffs gave way to concerns about how these relationships affected clients. Institutional change became as much a legitimate concern of caseworkers as individual change.

The neighborhood service centers made the most vital and significant contributions to the development of casework ideas and practices. A discussion of these centers will clarify what Service to Individuals and Families meant and the extent to which it affected and was affected by its clients.[8]

[8] The yearly budgets for the division were as follows: 1962–63, $379,-278.00; 1963–64, $620,367.00; 1964–65, $531,031.00; 1965–66, $602,972.00; 1966–67, $950,364.00. The figures do not include indirect costs for fiscal services, executive offices, public information, central services, personnel department and occupancy costs. Indirect costs averaged 25 percent per year. The National Institute of Mental Health, the City of New York, and the Office of Economic Opportunity were the major funding sources for the Service to Individuals and Families programs.

2

Neighborhood Service Centers

Hettie Jones

At the corner of Stanton and Ridge streets, toward the bottom of Manhattan Island, is a small store. On the door someone has scrawled "The Elegants," but the lettering on the window describes the place as Centro de Servicio al Vecindario, Neighborhood Service Center. A venetian blind on the inside of the door says "open/abierto" when the slats are turned one way and "closed/cerrado" when they are turned the other way. Even when the "closed" sign is out, though, people usually knock or try the door just to make sure.

Stanton and Ridge are narrow streets, so narrow that, even though the buildings rise no more than five stories, they seem to shut out the sky. If you look out the window from the waiting room of Neighborhood Service Center South, the whole street seems small and cramped. When the sofa and chairs are filled, there are cushions in the window, or in summer and spring you can sit on the one radiator. The workers' offices are not visible from the waiting room; they are tiny partitioned spaces, each large enough to hold a desk and chair for the worker and a chair for the client. If the client brings her children, as is often the case, they must sit on her lap or play on the floor or wander through the labyrinth of cubicles.

Appointments are not required here. When a client arrives, he is asked only his name. It was suggested at first that clients not be required to give their names directly upon presenting themselves, in order that the agency appear as nonbureaucratic as possible. But it soon became evident that it was not the giving of their names that mattered to people but the way in which they were asked for this information and the way the name was used or pronounced by those who had presumably come to serve the community.

In this center, as in the three others opened by MFY elsewhere in its service territory, the emphasis from the first was on the creation of an atmosphere of mutual respect in direct, daily contact with the people of the neighborhood. Within the context of respect, along with concrete aid such as homemaker help, legal assistance, emergency loans, etc., a social-casework approach was to be the major tenchnique of changing clients' ways of perceiving and responding to their circumstances. Like other aspects of MFY's activity, the neighborhood service centers were conceived as a way of reducing or eliminating self-defeating attitudes and behavior on the part of the urban poor.

Of course, many people in the urban slums *do* have severe emotional and psychological disturbances which render them functionally unable to take advantage of social, educational, or vocational opportunities. For most slum dwellers, however, self-defeating behavior is very largely a matter of economics, personal attitudes, and the limitations imposed by their life situation. Some people may defeat themselves because of simple lack of information. Services may be available somewhere in the community of which these people know nothing. Or self-defeating attitudes may develop and persist because people lack the basic skills for making an alternative adjustment—budgeting, purchasing, etc. Or people may suffer continuously because they do not have access to anyone with the power to intervene for them when they get into trouble with employers or schools or law-enforcement agencies. The neighborhood service centers were meant to provide significant, direct help with these problems while using such aid as the basis for ongoing casework counseling.

The Proposal justified the emphasis on concrete services as follows:

> Groups cannot be helped if they cannot be reached. It is generally conceded that lower class persons are drawn to agencies which

have concrete services to offer. Their social and economic problems are both concrete and overwhelming, and they are quite naturally in search of equally concrete ways of solving these problems. For another thing, they tend to define these problems as the consequences of external, arbitrary, capricious and malevolent forces. One detects in these groups powerful if subtle emphasis upon fate, upon the evil and immutable nature of man, upon man as the victim of superior or innate natural and social forces. For these and other reasons, members of these groups may regard the notion that a person in trouble can improve his circumstances through a better understanding of himself and the way in which he contributes to creating his own problems as alien and impractical.

A further reason for our emphasis upon concrete services is our conviction that such services, if imaginatively employed in the context of a casework relationship, can be a powerful force for change in human behavior. For one thing, services which relieve environmental pressures may thus release blocked energies for investment in areas of family and occupational activity which were previously neglected. Secondly, some persons who experience overwhelming environmental pressures may become capable of using specialized therapeutic relationships once the external pressures are reduced. What we wish to stress is the reconstruction of the individual's social conditions through a casework process so that he can then experience new pressures which exert a direct influence on him for change in a preconceived direction. We assume that significant social and psychological growth takes place as one becomes enmeshed in and is forced to grapple with changed social circumstances.[1]

The aim was something akin to a new casework. The centers, as we have noted, were to include an inquiry service, a liaison-resource service, and a social-planning service. The same social workers, conceived of as general practitioners, were to be responsible for all of the services, with the aid of appropriate consultants—lawyers, housing experts, etc. In addition, there was a projected category of under-one-roof services—a social caseworker, public-health nurse, visiting homemaker, escorts, and baby sitters—who were to provide the enabling social resources: the concrete services to relieve the environmental pressures that often prevented the social and psychological adjustment of deprived and overburdened people.

[1] *A Proposal for the Prevention and Control of Delinquency by Expanding Opportunities* (New York, Mobilization For Youth, 1961), pp. 356–57.

It was expected that the inquiry service would provide "immediate practical information in response to inquiries about housing, education, public welfare, legal problems, consumer problems, and the like." The liaison resource service, composed of representatives of various municipal departments and an employment service would rotate among the various centers and be available to anyone in case of emergency. The liaison personnel were to function as a team which, it was hoped, would relieve people of the strain of having to deal with many offices in connection with a single problem.

The social-planning service was projected essentially as a casework service for those who might benefit from a lengthy casework relationship. Emphasis would be on recognition and treatment of social as well as psychological problems, with appropriate attention to the cultural milieu of the client.

Early Problems

Neighborhood Service Center South (or No. 1) which opened on November 13, 1962, originally housed the staff of two neighborhood service centers plus a student unit. In early 1963, three more storefronts were opened, two south of Houston Street and one north.

The professional caseworkers who opened the first center, the branch director relates, had "different perceptions of what was to be accomplished . . . in a neighborhood service center," and most of their ideas were soon found to be "untrue or not feasible." The physical facilities were more cramped than anyone had anticipated, the staff (all professional) was considerably smaller, and none of the proposed under-one-roof services was available. A few weeks of formal and informal meetings and conferences served only to reveal the differences of opinion about what the casework role in such a setting was supposed to be, and how to deal with a population thought to be traumatized emotionally and psychologically.

For practical purposes, cases were classified in two ways. Social-broker cases were those which required immediate, concrete service. The term "broker" was not mentioned in the Proposal; in practice, however, it replaced the designation "generalist" or "general practitioner." Social-planning cases were those which required contact

with the client over a long period of time. However, the social
brokers were also the social planners, since all staff was required
to perform all the functions of the agency. The problem of labeling
the workers' role was part of the whole problem of defining service.

It became apparent, for example, early in the operation of the
neighborhood service centers that to provide a social-planning service for all the clients who needed it would not be possible with
the small staff available. After a few months, workers were allowed
to carry only 10 percent social-planning cases, the remainder being
broker cases. According to staff, however, the social-planning cases
sometimes differed little from the broker cases in the amount of the
worker's time and attention they required. By this time the word
was out: "Go to the NSC if you're in trouble."

A survey of NSC activities indicated that by early 1963 the
centers had already served more families and more individuals than
anyone had anticipated. From January 1 to April 1, 1963, 482
families were served and 3,833 acts of service rendered. This was
accomplished by a staff of ten.

What constituted an act of service? An office or field interview,
a home visit, a telephone discussion, correspondence with clients
or family or agency (public or private) or with another MFY
division. The same survey mentioned that "heavy amounts of time
are devoted to intervention for the satisfaction of basic survival requirements such as food, housing, and clothing." Workers, instruc-
ted to be available to all, were terribly overburdened, not only because of the large numbers of clients but also because most of the
clients had so many problems that it was difficult to know where
to begin. Mary Williams, a NSC worker, expressed some of this
frustration:

> I wonder if we can give the comprehensive, protracted services
> which deal with the many problems which prevail, one intensifying
> the other. Can we deal with the problems of substandard housing,
> medical, financial, recreational, and dietary needs? We attack one,
> perhaps two, of these problems, leaving others which are just as
> debilitating, eventually pulling the family back into preservice pat-
> terns and problems. After decades of deprivation, the deprived per-
> son is not necessarily impressed by the fact that his housing has

been improved if he continues to be hungry or poorly clothed. So much remains to be resolved. . . .[2]

It was obvious that, if any of the problems were to be solved, there would have to be some limitation on the service, to focus the program and to further refine the worker's role, but also to isolate what was most needed by the target population, or, as one director called it, "what it is that people suffer most about."

Soon after service was begun, it became evident that part of the responsibility for people's problems lay with the very institutions on which they had to rely for their existence. A good many clients lacked the basic survival requirements. Many people, whose welfare was supposed to be the responsibility of public agencies, were walking around in various states of crisis. Since, as we have noted, there had to be some limitation on the services offered by the centers, the Services to Individuals and Families administration decided that the neighborhood service centers would serve only clients with problems centering around the use of public and private agencies in the areas of welfare, health, education, housing, employment, and legal services. Those presenting other problems would be referred elsewhere for service. Whether a client was seen on a continuing basis or for merely brief contact was, then, no longer relevant; it was the nature of the problem, not of the client, that defined the duration of the contact.

An early series of taped interviews with workers and clients at one of the neighborhood service centers gives some idea of the reasons for this shift.

No one cares and you are like a stone on the sidewalk. What can you do if we are not lucky enough in the richest city in the world? We've got to go on welfare and have the welfare worker come up to see us and tell us how to live, and then she looks in the ice box at what we have. They want to know what kind of clothes you have, and when they see a telephone, they want to know who is paying for it and why that money isn't being used for food. They try every way to get you. They make it hard for you, and they don't

[2] Mary Williams, "Detailed Notes of a Professional Social Worker in a Mobilization For Youth Neighborhood Service Center" (mimeographed, New York Mobilization For Youth, undated), pp. 8–9.

want you to know from nothing. But they get a big salary every week. Before you get the first check, you wait three or four weeks, and when you get it, you don't know what to do first. They should have on their bones how much they give you. But you've got to make the best of it. One of these days I'll go up to the top of the Brooklyn Bridge, yell, "Here I go!" and then jump off. And you know what? Nobody will know! Nobody will care! Nobody will miss me.

Mr. L. had practically finished a TV repair course when illness intervened. He has not been able to afford the balance of the tuition and is now on welfare. Bitter and confused, he says, "Welfare won't pay for my schooling and if I pay ten dollars a week from what they give me, they'll close my case. But actually they'd save money by sending me to school, because then I could get a decent paying job and we wouldn't have to be on welfare. That's proof that they don't want you to get ahead. They want you to stay where you are."

Mr. R. complains about his slum tenement. "Every day when I come out of the building through a broken door and the filthy hall and see that abandoned car sitting in the garbage-littered snow, I feel as if I am living in a dump, one for which I am not responsible. I think to myself that the City of New York has abandoned me and my children, and I'm sad and ashamed. People who come to visit us look around with disgust and some have stopped coming. How can the city do this? It doesn't care about its residents or sanitation—not down here at least. But I've heard that it's different on Fifth Avenue. It's clean. The city thinks that something is being done because they have inspectors. But they don't know that the landlord pays off the health inspector or that the policeman on our beat lets the numbers man operate right out of our hall." [3]

The staffs had been engaged in a running battle with the Department of Welfare almost from the opening of the neighborhood service centers; this battle now took on larger and more consistent proportions. The policy of the centers toward the organizations and institutions they had to deal with mirrored the response of one client who said about Welfare: "They're quick to cut you off and slow

[3] Sherman Barr, "Poverty on the Lower East Side" (mimeographed, New York Mobilization For Youth, 1964).

to put you back on. When you're in need, the department takes its time, but when it's to their advantage, they can work fast. In other words, they can be efficient when they want to be."

Stabilization of the Program

By May 1963 it had become clear that many of the social-broker functions did not have to be handled by someone with a master's degree in social work, and a number of case aides were added to the staff. The liaison-resource service described in the Proposal was never put into effect, since the money allocated for it was used to hire additional case aides and caseworkers. In 1964 the Visiting Homemaker Service [4] was discontinued, and several of the home-makers were assigned to the neighborhood service centers to help in providing escort, translation, shopping, and other services.

By January 1964 the program of the neighborhood service centers had crystallized. The distinction between social-broker and social-planning cases in effect did not exist; there simply was no time for the long-term counseling envisioned in the Proposal for the social-planning cases. The Services to Individuals and Families divisional report of 1964 notes that limiting service to the provision of concrete aid in dealing with community agencies did not reduce the number of cases at the four centers. At that time the average case load per worker was thirty-two, and a client might be seen anywhere from one to five or six times a week. There was no question that the neighborhood service centers had reached the low-income population of the MFY area: Seventy-four percent of the cases were Puerto Rican, 20 percent Negro, 6 percent White. Seventy-five percent were known to the Department of Welfare, and 70 percent of the families were living in tenements.

A study commissioned by the Services to Individuals and Families chief to clarify the program called for "systematic cultivation of the welfare 'generalist' who is a resource specialist, mediator, service supplier, coordinator, caseworker, group worker, community organization worker, housing and welfare expert, social action specialist and diplomatic envoy with the establishment at one and

[4] See chapter on "The Use of Indigenous Personnel" in this volume for a description of this program.

the same time." [5] The role of the caseworker in practice was quite as complex as that outlined above but it was less than systematically cultivated.

In rendering concrete service, the worker acted in any one or a combination of several roles. People who came to the NSC became dependent on their workers to intervene for them with the service systems (Welfare mainly); workers performed this intervention over and over, acting in behalf of the client instead of enabling the client to make the necessary connections himself. There was too little time, and there were too many clients, for the service to be directed more consciously toward overcoming self-defeating behavior. In addition, there was a new awareness on the part of the workers of where the fault really lay; they questioned whether changing the client's behavior was possible or necessary, given what they had learned about their clients and the service systems with which they were in steady contact.

Mary Williams summed up these ideas as follows:

We observe the phenomena of dependency and denial on many avenues of service, and it may, in part, account for the difficulty deprived persons have in accurately assessing or accepting the planful roles they need to play to break the chain of circumstances by which they are surrounded. Accompanying this is the fact that their appraisal of [social systems] which have operated to freeze them into a given socio-economic mold, which . . . in turn establish the bulk of their life experience . . . leads them to the . . . denial-projection mechanism. For, in fact, they have demonstrable evidence which supports their [feeling of] blamelessness. . . .

Enhancing the blameless-helpless-hopeless syndrome are daily encounters with systems which appear more concerned with smooth operational procedures than the needs of the deprived. The denigrating responses of the systems' reactions to the problems and needs of the deprived may be discerned when a welfare investigator curtly replies, "I'm too busy to send you clothing"; when the hospital admonishes them to be there at 9:00 A.M., only to keep them waiting until 2:00 P.M. for the doctor; when the dietician "hasn't

[5] Frances G. King, *A Study of Services to Individuals and Families Within Mobilization For Youth,* (New York, Mobilization For Youth, 1963), p. 41.

gotten a chance to send special diet forms to welfare"; when they receive no response whatever to complaints made to a city building department; when the landlord never seems able to get around to repairing the plumbing, the rat holes, the radiators, or the windows; when a new employee is hired, in the same job classification, and earns more than those with tenure (and a Spanish accent); when UIB [Unemployment Insurance Board] summarily denies benefits because the employer, who forced them to resign, describes them as an "involuntarily quit"; when the health station is seldom clear about why they must make tedious arrangements for the care of the other children in order to take one child in for what looks like a "weigh in"; when the teacher berates them about their "lack of interest" in Johnnie's reading problems when managing the problem of feeding and clothing Johnnie seems to be quite enough for them to handle; when there just isn't time for the "free lawyer" to explain to them exactly how it is that Joe, who's been in jail for three months, hasn't been sentenced yet; when everyone tells them not to pay exorbitant credit charges yet they can most easily secure credit in times of need only from those vendors whose credit charges are exorbitant; when they come to New York City in pursuit of "the American Dream" only to be told that they are "undeserving" and must return to the place of their legal residence; or, when welfare insists that employed teen-agers, whose hope for an improved existence has not been destroyed, contribute the lion's share of earnings toward the support of the family.

To draw this together, I would submit that there is an apparent consistency between the world of the deprived and their perceptions of it as a hostile, withholding, powerful, aggressive milieu in which they must fashion firm, pragmatic, self-protective coping devices to survive in this milieu. Unfortunately, the coping devices may be largely self-defeating.[6]

6 Mary Williams, "Direct Work With the Severely Deprived: Some Basic Considerations "(mimeographed, New York, Mobilization For Youth, 1964), pp. 4–6. She continues: "These devices include dodging the corner grocer to take their credit to another grocer, moving before rent is due in order to enjoy some 'extra' monies, selling their furniture and telling welfare that it was repossesed and must be replaced, throwing a 'rent party,' going to the local bar with the last $3.00 '. . . 'cause everybody eats somehow'; giving up a plan for marriage because 'at least welfare sends the money regular', applying home remedies except when there is no choice but to seek medical attention, and moving from one extra-legal marital relationship to another. . . . This apparent fluidity and 'dealing' appears to contribute to the emergent or survival nature of the requests presented to

If the neighborhood service centers had had the facilities and the staff to provide each client with an extended casework relationship, some have contended, a new kind of casework could have been devised. Yet it is more likely that such a casework could only be developed when caseworkers can get the series of systems, which now fail to maintain people adequately, to respond to their needs. Since at that time, this was not possible, workers were urged to abandon the psychological side of casework services.[7]

The planned rectification of self-defeating patterns of behavior through psychotherapeutic techniques and environmental manipulation simply had to take a back seat. The individual's motivation to change his life hardly matters if a rat is scampering over his feet. A mother cannot be expected to bring her child to school if the child has no shoes. And most of the time neither the rat-infested apartment nor a lack of shoes is due to client behavior.

Workers still gave some psychological help to some clients, but by and large they were not expected to do so. The emphasis was on giving service related to the basic matters of existence. An important aspect of this decision, which has had far-reaching consequences, was the conviction that the good adjustment of NSC clients would have meant a good adjustment to poverty and to the constant violation of their rights by community agencies. The need for choice was clear, and the choice that was made was clearly the only one to be made in the circumstances, at that time, by socially conscious people.

The Role of the Advocate

By mid-1964 the social workers in the neighborhood service centers had assumed the title "advocate." The title reflected less a

---

the practitioner. By the time the problems are presented . . . the situation has so deteriorated that the deprived view immediate service as essential. . . . The sense of blamelessness appears to contribute to their sense of helplessness and hopelessness. These compound entrapments appear to damage clearly feelings of security and compromise greatly an investment in planful activity."

[7] The provision of psychological services, for which there is still a very great need, is discussed in the paper "Psychological Help for the Poor" in this volume.

method than an attitude, a stance. For people had begun to see the
NSC as their sole means, not only of communicating with service
institutions but of obtaining a measure of justice from them. They
had become aware that it was possible to gain access to power—
power they did not view themselves as possessing—to confront an
institution which was depriving them of their rights. Quite simply,
it was a great relief to many people to be able to go somewhere
where a phone call would be made that literally meant the difference
between suffering and the cessation of suffering for a period of
time.

Consider the following two cases, which are not atypical of life
on the Lower East Side:

A fifty-four-year-old woman has been living in her one-room flat
for three months with no lights. She cannot pay the electric bill,
and the Department of Welfare, even after repeated requests, will
not put her on its rolls because she cannot establish the legitimacy
of her New York residence to its satisfaction. One day she complains
of feeling ill and goes to the hospital; the hospital sends her home.
She goes again when, after a few days, she feels worse, and is again
sent home. Nothing is wrong; nothing shows on the x-rays. Three
days later she returns to the hospital with a worker from NSC
South. It is now noticed that the woman has a large tumor in her
chest and is dying of bone cancer. Is it the three day's wait that
has located the illness or the magic of the worker's demand, the
power she wields as the representative of a social agency? And on
whose conscience do those three months of darkness lie?

A woman whose son has been wounded in Vietnam wants to find
out where he is and how he is. She has no address; she knows only
that he has been taken from the Philippines to a hospital in Japan.
She calls the Red Cross and is told that it is not possible to obtain
such information. She comes to NSC South. A worker phones the
Red Cross for her and is given an address to which one may write
for the desired information. Where is the magic this time? Where
is the failure?

Advocacy, as applied to a social worker, has been defined as the
willingness to intervene with a government agency on behalf of a
low-income person. It does not mean helping the poor man to help

himself or enabling him to better manage his transactions with the governmental department. It means filling in the power deficit on his side of the transaction by providing him with a defender who has specialized knowledge of the rules and regulations of the system. (This includes its informal and therefore unstated inner workings, which may be of major significance in how decisions get made and how they can get changed.) But most of all advocacy means a readiness to become an adversary, to pit oneself against the system with whatever means are at hand, whether persuasion, manipulation, or straightforward pressure.[8]

Relative to their advocate designation, workers were called upon to promote institutional change, with the Department of Welfare as the special target. Their methods and techniques were essentially the same as those conventionally called upon to effect bureaucratic change. There are the telephone and the letter, irritation on single cases. There is the more direct pressure of walking in a picket line in front of welfare headquarters, along with welfare recipients, to demand larger school-clothing allotments.

Sherman Barr, director of the neighborhood-service-center program, has referred to the advocate as a gadfly. This is a very adequate metaphor if one sees institutions that serve the poor as a herd of immobile cattle faced with the problem of a lot of sudden bites. When the animal finally realizes that no amount of tail-switching is going to do away with the irritation, he just may reason that it would be better to change position or deal with the problem another way. (Services to Individuals and Families was sometimes asked by such institutions: Why don't you people behave like other agencies? Why don't you be good and stop bothering me?) [9]

[8] Richard M. Elman, "Neighborhood Service Centers" (mimeographed, New York, Mobilization For Youth, undated), p. 41. From Mobilization, the concept of a neighborhood service center assuming an advocacy stance on behalf of clients spread through New York City and the country.

[9] Agency personnel often complained bitterly that MFY clients were lying and cheating. There is little doubt that in some instances they were correct. But as Sherman Barr has pointed out (*op. cit.*, p. 11), "The poor do not and cannot understand bureaucratic problems. Use of the Welfare Department requires a level of knowledge and sophistication which is impossible for the bulk of the poor to learn and employ. For instance, the concept of appeal is unheard of. Service systems are seen by the poor as systems which must be manipulated if decent service is to be obtained.

The advocate worker had to amass a considerable array of information on community resources, more than would suffice for a worker in a traditional family-service agency. A few workers became experts in housing or in health; everyone had to have a special knowledge of welfare. With regard to welfare, in fact, SIF innovated a welfare bulletin which was kept absolutely up-to-date by an experienced consultant. Thanks to the bulletin, NSC workers often had information in advance of Department of Welfare workers themselves—some of whom, as time passed, would call to find out the latest regulations. This bulletin became in great demand all over the city and country, as did information on the advocate role.

The public image of the NSC worker as advocate has refined relations with the Department of Welfare and, to a lesser degree, with other institutions. Since the emphasis is on rights rather than on undue demands, certain channels have been created, and a measure of understanding has been arrived at through negotiation as well as pressure. MFY Legal Services Unit has also been involved in dealings with the Department of Welfare, and this social worker–lawyer alignment has been invaluable.[10]

Later Developments

From October 1962 through March 1965, the SIF program served 18,500 persons (16 percent of the total MFY-area population) in 3,700 families. In mid-1965, in order to provide more effective service, two centers were closed and their staff redistributed to NSC's South and North.[11]

As the months passed, it became clear that the advocacy stance of the workers was successful in achieving concrete gains for the

Methods and techniques for beating the system are disseminated." Mobilization's point of view was that, if the system were operating correctly, there would be a lot less cheating. Dealing with the problem on a client-by-client basis would only be attacking the effect and not the cause.

[10] See the chapter on, "Legal Challenges to Formal and Informal Denial of Welfare Rights" in Vol. 4, *Justice and the Law*.

[11] The space already secured in one of the area's low-income housing projects, which became NSC North, was the first nonstorefront center to be put in operation. By this time, however, the lack of "visibility" made little difference. Within a short time NSC North had many more cases than had been anticipated.

vast majority of clients, but was not particularly useful in bringing about broad changes in the policy of the Department of Welfare. At this point the decision was made to organize groups of clients to seek changes in the department's procedures and policies through concerted community action.[12] The reason for this partial shift in emphasis in the neighborhood service centers was twofold. First, staff was convinced that such action was necessary if bureaucratic service institutions were to be made more responsive to people's needs. Second, there was the desire to experiment with implementing the hypothesis that participation in social action is therapeutic to the client.

In December 1965, the policy was instituted to gear intake more sharply to public-welfare concerns. Workers were advised that in no case should they "spend an inordinate amount of time on areas not related to income maintenance, health, safety, housing, and concrete problems of welfare clients." In addition, the out-of-area cases, which had formerly constituted 15 percent of the total caseload, were closed and no more out-of-area cases were to be accepted without supervisory approval. With the availability of additional funds a third center was opened in 1966 (NSC West), located in three small storefronts. In addition to the service provided in the other two centers, NSC West provided adult employment counseling.

Range of Services

Although the emphasis in the neighborhood service centers has been increasingly geared toward welfare problems, considerable assistance has been rendered in other areas.

In 1966, a public-health nurse was hired to provide group-teaching services to staff and clients, make home visits in emergencies, interpret and follow up treatment plans with clients, and intervene on behalf of staff with clinics and hospitals.

Active and aggressive intervention by NSC staff saved several clients from being hastily and incorrectly admitted to mental wards,

[12] The chapter on "Organizations of Welfare Clients" in Vol. 2, *Community Development,* describes the history of these organizations in detail.

saw to it that children of tubercular mothers were x-rayed without the usual delay, and forced reevaluation of hasty judgments about retardation, thus avoiding unnecessary institutional commitment.

Ancillary services were provided to make medical care possible. MFY escorts helped get frightened clients to clinics and interpreted the medical situation and hospital structure. Hundreds of dollars were made available annually, specifically for use as carfare to take young children to clinics or make regular visits to a prenatal clinic. Funds were also granted for eyeglasses, summer-camp physical examinations, emergency dental care, and the like when it became apparent that unreasonable delays would further increase social disorganization in the family and deterioration in the health situation of the client—particularly the young child.

The child-care service provided short-term baby-sitting while mothers were away from their homes for any number of reasons. This brief relief for the mother went far toward lessening the tensions and strains of everyday living. Although the service was essentially custodial, this service was used to uncover unmet needs. It was surprising and shocking to find children under the age of three who were legally blind or almost deaf or retarded and whose parents were not aware of the situation. Child care also enhanced the use the mother made of clinic visits. Placing well children in the care station during such a visit enabled a mother to give individualized attention to a sick child and eliminated the psychological wear and tear of disciplining children in the difficult environment of a clinic waiting room.

The services provided in relation to housing were also notable. Staff filled out scores of applications for low-cost housing projects and attempted to interpret the many confusing reasons given for rejections. A very important aspect of housing work related to the Department of Welfare. Workers took a strong stand to insure that the department moved quickly to provide security deposits and rent when an opening did become available for housing. Quick action often made the difference between a family's success or failure in securing a new apartment.

And finally the center staff served as friends and neighbors to the community:

Working mothers leave keys for their children; dogs are kept for short periods of time; addicts drop in to sleep off a high; emergency first aid is dispensed; money is held for clients who are afraid of being burglarized; policemen stop in for a cup of coffee; derelicts drop by to sit in the air-conditioned lobby during the summer; children drop in for a dime to buy some soda pop on a hot day; delinquent-prone youngsters check with us on the wisdom of "copping a plea" or going to trial; people drop in and preface their remarks by saying, "They told me that if you couldn't help me, no one could." [13]

The NSC Experience

From one point of view the neighborhood service centers can be regarded as a return to the political clubhouse style of help, with social workers instead of politicians dispensing the aid. From another point of view, they went far beyond the clubhouse into the realm of the institutional ombudsman, functioning as the watchdogs of public agencies.

A new casework, however, was not developed. In an early appraisal of the centers it was felt:

> The casual voluntaristic nature of the present neighborhood service center program (largely walk-ins and informal referrals) precludes any systematic appraisal of the entire family in its total situation. Although gains doubtless have been achieved with these clients through the provision of concrete services . . . serious problems continue in many of these families, gains tend to be lost, and some of the children become progressively more endangered. These outcomes would suggest that the segmented, crisis-oriented approach may not be the method of choice for families entrenched in the poverty status.[14]

Several factors accounted for the lack of development of the new casework. First, by agreeing to meet the needs of the clients

[13] Excerpted from Sherman Barr, "New Directions in Social and Medical Services for Young Children: A Review of the Mobilization For Youth Program," paper presented at the Conference on Changing Patterns of Health Services for Preschool Children (mimeographed, University of Minnesota, September 1965), pp. 19–24.

[14] Freda Taran, "Neighborhood Service Centers" (New York, Mobilization For Youth, undated), p. 7.

as they themselves defined them, the centers soon became bogged down in giving service. Available staff time was insufficient to develop casework relationships. Second, and more important, Mobilization consciously chose to demonstrate how inadequately the institutions of society were functioning for poor people. Thus the concern of the centers was with institutional rather than personal change.

At a certain level of poverty, the demands of merely staying alive are so great and overwhelming that an attempt to form a psychologically oriented therapeutic relationship has little chance of success without the provision of concrete services. Since the centers wanted to serve as many people as possible (and had to depend on other institutions, like the Welfare Department, which controlled the significant concrete resources), there was neither the time nor the real possibility of developing the new casework techniques as originally intended.[15]

It is also reasonable to conclude that many people could have benefited from efforts to teach them to advocate for themselves. Some workers feel that advocacy puts the client on a treadmill: With such help readily available he will simply keep returning without ever attempting to assume an advocate stance himself. Others feel that advocacy is necessary, that clients will change only when the system is changed and until then will keep needing this help. Beyond a few individual workers' experiments, there were no systematic attempts to develop new methods and techniques for working with multiproblem families who might be involved in a casework relationship. Except for channeling clients to the welfare groups—which worked well—no systematic attempts were made to involve clients in advocacy or to train them to act as advocates for themselves.[16] That the neighborhood service centers' advocacy

[15] It is also clear that the agency underestimated the difficulty of the task, first in not acknowledging the degree of training and conceptual ability required of staff for the task as well as its ability to restrict service to provide time to do the conceptual job.

[16] Of course, many clients learned how to advocate for themselves just by observing the workers. And most workers tended to urge clients to try to advocate for themselves. But to be effective, advocacy must be backed up by power. Clients, acting alone, do not have the power to secure their legitimate demands when these are arbitrarily denied. The caseworker could threaten and follow through with picketing, legal action, etc.

for their clients has created dependency is arguable. The risk of giving help is dependency. It is reasonable not to worry about this risk until clients are no longer faced with the broader risks of lack of food, clothing, and shelter.

The case record of Mrs. J. speaks to the point:

Mr. J. works and is out of the home from 8:00 A.M. to 6:00 P.M. Mrs. J. works and is out of the home from 5:00 P.M. to 11:00 P.M. From 5:00 P.M. to 6:00 P.M. the eight children are scheduled, in Mrs. J.'s words, "like the Marine Corps." The rest of her life is just as disciplined. She knows exactly which door to use in which department store on which day for which purpose. She travels from the Bronx to Brooklyn to save a few pennies on meat. She knows personally the owner of every second-hand clothing store on the Lower East Side. Her sons get their haircuts at the Bowery barber schools, where she saves one dollar over the regular price. She would never move from her small apartment to a different project because she is now living adjacent to a middle-income development populated largely by Jews, and where the Jews are, she says, you can find better schools, better police protection, better shopping, better recreation, and better support for various civic improvements. She knows which police station to go to for Christmas toys, which social agency for money, and which church offers more clothing. . . . In other words, she is everything some people in our society want poor people to be, thrifty, disciplined, and organized. However, after the seventh interview, she blurted out that all wasn't what it appeared to be. Occasionally she and her husband engage in violent battles which sometimes result in the police being called in. "Something has to give," she said, "something just has to give." [17]

Another projected intention for the neighborhood service centers was not realized—that the centers would coordinate the efforts of a variety of agencies and institutions into a coherent neighborhood service system. The liaison unit of city-agency personnel was never put into operation. By becoming advocates the center staffs became engaged in controversy, and this made cooperation—as envisioned in the idea of the liaison unit—impossible. But it seems likely that at the time the centers would have achieved a good deal less with

[17] Barr, *op. cit.*, p. 6.

most institutions had they avoided controversy and used friendly persuasion.

By the spring of 1966, the neighborhod service centers had four identifiable functions: (1) to provide information and referral services to assist people in the use of established agencies; (2) to act as an advocate to protect the client's interests and rights with respect to other agencies and to seek changes in those agencies' procedural policies that will become precedents for similar situations; (3) to provide concrete services directly to individuals and families; and (4) to organize and mobilize groups for collective action on behalf of the residents of the neighborhood.[18]

The Perlman-Jones report on the NSC's, compiled for the Department of Health, Education and Welfare, concludes with the following admonition:

> It is important to recognize the limitations of neighborhood service centers in order to grasp what their appropriate role can be. At present they are being expected to compensate for and bring about changes in social conditions and social services, tasks which are beyond their unaided resources. They are, in effect if not in intention, being used as a way of avoiding the more radical action concerning social conditions and social provisions which the situation now requires. In the future they can take a more modest place as an essential part of a system of basic social provisions which insures humane and effective help to all people.[19]

While Perlman and Jones are correct in writing that the more adequate provision of services deals only with the effects of poverty and will not change its causes, the neigbhorhood service centers have provided a base from which social-action organization can agitate for more basic changes. In any event, it is clear that, given the nature of the various institutional bureaucracies with which the poor must interact, there is a compelling need for a neighborhood-service-center operation which carries on an information-giving as

18 Robert Perlman and David Jones, *Neighborhood Service Centers* (Washington, D.C., Department of Health, Education and Welfare, 1967), p. 1.
19 *Ibid.*, p. 80.

well as an advocacy function for clients.[20] Certainly every settlement house in the country, as well as every citizens' organization located in a low-income area, should have a neighborhood service center.

One of the case aides characterized NSC clients as follows: "A third need only information, a third need support and advocacy, and a third need long-term counseling." Low-income areas are in great need of a dependable, available source for information, advocacy, counseling, and social action, buttressed by such concrete services as baby-sitting, homemaking, escort, legal aid, and emergency loans.

In less than five years of operation, (October 1962 to June 1967), the centers served 43,064 individuals in 10,487 families. Some 70 percent of the presenting problems involved the Welfare Department. The majority of problems were related to residents' eligibility, unmet needs—including clothing, household goods, beds and bedding—inadequate allowance for family size, late checks, incorrect computation, unserved cases, no worker for several months. About 40 percent of those who had welfare problems also had problems involving housing, health, schools, courts, etc. The remaining 30 percent of nonwelfare problems were roughly divided into school, health, and a miscellaneous category including addiction, employment, child neglect, emotional illness, housing, and housekeeping.

The amount of help these figures indicate is staggering, especially when one considers that most of it would not have been available had the service centers not been in operation. Without question, the neighborhood service centers discovered a vast pool of need which society's welfare institutions had been ignoring—largely because those institutions had been permitted to develop their policies and procedures with little or no accountability to the clients whom they served. The NSCs provided the means to begin a reversal of this process.

[20] The dramatic decrease in rejections for home relief in New York City from 66 percent in 1962 to 31 percent in 1967 is clear evidence of the need for these centers.

3

The Social Agency as a Disseminator of Information

Sherman Barr

When Mobilization For Youth began its operations there was much evidence that settlement houses, hospitals, schools, and other established social agencies on the Lower East Side were not perceived, by low-income people or by the agencies themselves, as sources of information relevant to the lives of the poor. If a resident wanted information about welfare, for example, he would rely on the community grapevine; it would never occur to him to go to an agency. Now, five years later, these agencies are clamoring to get more information so that they can dispense it to the population they serve.

The limited success of these agencies in information dissemination was demonstrated by the adult survey of the neighborhood carried out in 1961.[1]

Do you know of any neighborhood organizations or local groups that are trying to do something about problems in the area:

No: don't know of any such organizations	681
Yes: Lower East Side Neighborhoods Association	81
Two Bridges Council; Good Neighbors	23
Tenants' councils and block associations	48
Settlement houses and community centers	140
Churches	55

[1] *Adult Survey Code Book,* Vol. 1, (New York, Mobilization For Youth, 1962).

Schools; PTA's; Board of Education   37
Local political clubs   27
Other organizations   61
Know of some but can't name them   17
                                                      ─────
                                                      1,170

When you have a difficult personal or family problem who are you most likely to talk it over with:

Husband or wife   337
Brothers or sisters; brothers-in-law or sisters-in law living
  in household   86
Children   86
Parents or parents-in-law; grandparents   69
Other relatives   53
Friends   98
Social worker; welfare worker; city state or private
  agency   37
Other professional (i.e. doctor, lawyer, counselor)   79
No one; myself; person having difficulty with   120
Don't know; vague irrelevant answer; no answer   19
                                                       ─────
                                                        988

The problem of lack of information became apparent very early in the program. Large numbers of people came in for help with problems which can be solved rather easily by supplying information. One frequently heard such questions as, is it true that . . . where can I find . . . someone told me that . . . I heard. . . .

The Use of Information

The problem of disseminating information to the poor often devolves to their inability to use information that they have been given. For example, a client may be unable to use what he knows about a clinic or some other kind of service; he lacks the financial wherewithal to do so—perhaps carfare to get to the service or the very small fee connected to it. In time the information itself is regarded as irrelevant. The lack of child-care facilities also may prevent use of information or of a service. Telling a mother that the

prenatal clinic at Beth Israel Hospital meets at 8:30 is rather use-
less unless arrangments have been made to care for her preschool
children while she is at the clinic.

People often fail to use information because they do not understand it. Information is often given rather quickly, with the assumption that clients understand what is being said and can really
follow through. For example, a client may be told, "Okay, go to Welfare, you seem to be eligible; the center is at Fifth Street and bring
this paper, that paper, that paper, this paper, the other paper, in
order to do this, in order to do that." The client will simply nod
his head and leave without admitting that he does not completely
understand. Sometimes the information given is simply not accurate; after trial and error and frustration, people do not return
to the source to get correct information, because they assume that
the first negative experience is typical.

Still another factor preventing proper use of information is the
transportation system; information has to be very precise, and maps
or other directions given so that a person who does not understand
English well can find his way. Frequently information is not given
concerning geographical boundaries, how much time might be involved, or what telephone numbers to check. A physical orientation to an agency is sometimes necessary as part of the information
picture. For instance, it is not helpful merely to tell a client to go
to Bellevue Hospital. Bellevue is a complex of buildings which can
be overwhelming to the ordinary citizen, let alone those who lack
the necessary language skills. A client might go there, look at the
place, and come back much too frightened to use it.

The information supplied by the local culture is very often in
contradiction to what the social agency says. A worker may say,
"Go to Welfare, they'll take care of you," but a friend in the community tells the client: "Welfare is a bunch of dogs, they won't
treat you right, and they'll insult you; you shouldn't go there because no one will help you anyway." Or the community may offer
him crippling misinformation, such as these remarks by the father
of six children, who received Aid to Dependent Children funds:

I never complain about anything to Welfare. The more you complain, the more angry they get. And the investigator gets $50 every

time he closes a case, so he's going to cut you off if you complain too much. I shut up and just take it.

The same situation occurs often with medical facilities; the informal communication links take over and prevent adequate use of information. Good information-giving techniques have to anticipate such a situation and the client's problems, bring them out into the open, and help the client deal with them so that proper use can be made of information.

In terms of transmission of information, it is important not only to say just what the service is and what time to get there but also to warn the client of some of the problems he may meet—a snippy clerk, a cold official, an elevator operator who gives vague directions.

Information about social security or veteran's benefits is given in subway placards; other kinds of public benefits are advertised on television and in periodicals. This is not true in regard to most medical services, and certainly not to welfare services and education services. There appears to be an inclination to hold back information in the fear that extensive dissemination will result in a flood of applicants for the services, and thus will involve additional expenditures which the agency cannot afford.

Some people who have been on welfare for many years do not know what to do about eviction notices, utility bills, special clothing needs, and the like; it is obvious that information has not been shared. In case after case, the sharing of information by the Welfare Department would, indeed, result in a run on the services and tremendous expense. For example, although the manual states that the welfare recipient is supposed to have a minimum standard of furniture, clothing, and household equipment, this information is not given to him. As a matter of fact, if the client doesn't ask, the Welfare Department doesn't offer.

Regarding education, how many parents know what topics the teacher is supposed to cover over a period of time, or where they can go to protest a decision to put a child in a special class or in a 600 school for problem children? This sort of information is seldom shared with parents in other than crisis situations. By and large, the client gets to know what the agency wants him to know;

beyond that he must rely on his own wits and on gossip within the community. Information obtained in this way is frequently inaccurate and may be damaging.

Information and Action

The decision of an agency to give information and to provide the means for the clients to follow through on it implies that the agency has adopted a certain stance toward action. If it deliberately chooses to provide information about welfare which will increase the demands made on the welfare system and the amount of expenditure expected of it, that agency is not only providing more information to clients but is also taking the risk of creating problems in its relationship with the welfare system itself.

In its attitude toward providing information, an agency reflects its philosophy, its preferred clientele, and the kind of risks it is willing to take. If a clinic meets at an inconvenient hour, would it not be the responsibility of the agency providing the information to help clients organize to change the meeting time? In other words, where does the job of giving information develop into the job of counseling action? Or again, if the agency tells a client about a particular service and the service agency does not perform as expected, what responsibility does the worker or his agency have to do something about it? Clearly, good information requires a certain commitment, a certain stance on the part of the agency. A client seeking help in applying for public assistance said about a previous experience:

> Miss K., the social worker, gave us a letter to take to Welfare. If she had gone with us instead of just writing a letter, it would have been different. If you go alone, they treat you one way. But if you go with somebody from an organization, they treat you another way. She's very nice, Miss K., but I don't know what she's going to do for me. She looks at me, smiles and says, "Hm-um. Hm-um." Well, life just isn't that calm for us.

One well-known service agency has never given information concerning minimum standards or the right to appeal decisions of the Department of Welfare. Prior to the institution of Mobilization's services, only a handful of appeals had been made to the State Department of Social Welfare. Such fair hearings are now requested by the hundreds.

To obtain information for a client from the Board of Education, the social worker may have to use the legal service or some other weapon to force the information from the educational system. The reason people have not identified social-work agencies as places which hold information is not because of the agencies' unwillingness to transmit information, but because of their unwillingness to go to bat for the client in order to make sure the information is obtained and put to good use.

Information and the Image of the Social Agency

The image of a social agency in the client's mind is crucial. For example, a publicity campaign was carried out by a neighborhood legal services unit in a large eastern city. The area was blanketed with notices announcing meetings, and lawyers were sent around to speak with local groups. The net result of all this effort was not any marked increase in the number of people using these services. Eventually it was discovered that the neighborhood legal service unit was not accepting any criminal cases. Since there was a great need for help in the criminal courts in this particular neighborhood, legal service had taken on a negative image—it simply wasn't viewed as a place where one could get help. As a result, the legal services which were provided were not fully utilized.

Mobilization has discovered that word of mouth is probably the best and most common means of transmitting information in a slum; mimeographed releases or sound trucks alone are not enough. Attendance at meetings of neighborhood organizations also helps to open up communication links. But what really paves the way to communication is long and persistent work to develop an image of an organization which the clients value and discuss with respect among themselves. Eighty-five percent of the new cases at MFY's neighborhood service centers are referred through word-of-mouth techniques, and the very successful welfare groups have developed primarily through word of mouth.

An interesting illustration of image as a factor in the dissemination of information occurred in the first local campaign around Operation Head Start. About ten summer workers and Vista volunteers were employed in a crash program to enlist youngsters in the program. Circulars were distributed, tables were set up on every street corner, sound trucks were used, workers approached people on the streets and on the stoops, they filled mailboxes and so on, but the response was very limited; many openings in the program were not filled. The following year registration was far better. Some of this improvement may be attributed to the use of better techniques throughout the city, but it is also true that Mobilization had improved its name and image in the area by making more services and information available. Since Mobilization was a source of information about Head Start, people were more receptive to such information.

Regarding the information provided by the neighborhood service centers, one of the psychiatric consultants observed that there was what he called a "place transference." Information or suggestions coming from neighborhood-service-center workers were especially valued because their source was the neighborhood service center. The image had been enhanced over the years, and thus information was shared and used much more broadly.

In the current cold war, jamming of radio frequencies is a much used tactic to prevent information from being used. MFY has sought to unjam the client's receivers by providing clear information and making sure that the information can be acted on, either by providing the needed ancillary services—e.g., day care—or by pressuring institutions to act, by insisting that institutions expand the information they transmit and cut down on conflicting messages and discordant techniques of dissemination, and by developing the image of MFY as a helping institution.

One of the major roles of voluntary social agencies is to act as watchdogs of the public agencies. Private agencies not only must give information to clients about the public agencies but also must make certain that public bodies are accountable to their clients. Private social agencies are admirably suited to do this since they depend on public bodies for neither funds nor legitimacy. They can both organize clients to seek their rights and arouse public opinion. They cannot really be effective in providing information unless they act as the champions and advocates of client needs. For it is not information alone that clients need but also the ability to use it.

4

The Use of Indigenous Personnel as Service Givers

Hettie Jones

MFY program designers knew that if the agency's services were to be used fully, its staff would need interpreters and guides who could explain the slum to them and, just as important, explain their presence to the slum. To serve this dual function, the project undertook to hire a number of indigenous personnel—local people who presumably could communicate with both the neighborhood and the agency.

The idea of using neighborhood people in social service is not new. Indigenous personnel had been used earlier by social agencies in New York and other large cities, by school systems, and in work with juvenile gangs. Settlement workers in the early part of this century used such persons as translators to help them in their work with the foreign-born.

A number of reasons were given for using indigenous personnel in addition to the neighborhood bridge function they were expected to serve. Expanded programs for the poor had produced a great many job openings, but relatively few middle-class professionals were willing or available to work with lower-class clients; hiring neighborhood people to work in these programs was a way of attacking the problem of staff shortage. Involving the poor in gainful employment would work directly to reduce poverty. Finally, those employed would serve as excellent and noticeable models for the rest of the community. In MFY's case, the bridge or interpreter function was, at least at first, the most important in-view of the very real language and cultural barrier that separated most of the professionals from their largely Spanish-speaking clientele.

It was realized that not all lower-class residents of the area could perform this function. Some would be too hostile toward social-welfare agencies; others might not actually represent the interests of lower-class people, being themselves on their way up the social ladder. Still others would simply not have the intellectual, verbal, or emotional capacities to do the work.

In addition to the problem of selecting the proper people for these jobs, there was the problem of how to train them. Indigenous personnel had to be trained and yet remain essentially who they were; any training that took them out of their lower-class status might eliminate the major part of their usefulness. For example, if their attitudes about the neighborhood were drastically changed, would they be able to convey to the agency the opinions of the population to be served? (Asked to rate the Lower East Side as a place to live, 70.5 percent of the MFY professional staff called it poor or very poor, but only 37.5 percent of the indigenous staff and 34.4 of the community rated it so.[1])

The intent, obviously, was not to make a colonial service of these people, thereby destroying their native roots. To the contrary, their roots in the neighborhood were expected "to attract other impoverished persons who ordinarily avoid social services . . . encourage the development of services meaningful to these persons, and . . . bring about their active involvement in individual and collective problem solving." [2]

The first and most important use of indigenous personnel within Services to Individuals and Families was in the Visiting Homemaker Service. The purpose of this service, as envisioned in the Proposal, was to "facilitate the acculturation of newcomers to the project area and to intervene in families in which self-defeating life styles have been perpetuated for generations." This was to be

[1] Charles Grosser, "Middle Class Professionals . . . Lower Class Clients" (unpublished dissertation, Columbia University School of Social Work, 1965), pp. 88–89.
[2] George Brager, "The Low-Income Nonprofessional, an Overview of His Role in Program" (mimeographed, New York, Mobilization for Youth, 1964), p. 11.

accomplished by providing a "corps of practical home-service workers" who were to offer "both training and assistance, as needed." Homemakers were to be recruited from "a cultural, socio-economic, and ethnic background similar to that of the resident population, with a high-school degree or equivalent education." Preferably, they were to come from the Lower East Side, so that they might have a thorough knowledge of conditions in this area.

Their role was not seen as merely that of a temporary housekeeper (such as those employed by the Department of Welfare for emergency care when a mother is temporarily out of the home), although they might perform housekeeping duties at times. Rather, they were to be instructor-demonstrators, offering support and assistance in home management and family life and encouraging the use of other resources available through MFY—rather like the kindly neighbor lady from down the block who offers home-grown knowledge from her own backyard of experience along with her favorite recipe for strawberry jam. But all this was to take place in the slum, the advice-giver has probably been on welfare herself, and the recipe would be for the use of government-surplus powdered milk. Later reports of clients' perceptions of the homemaker staff verify that they were indeed seen as "neighbors, perhaps a little better off, but nonetheless persons with whom one reciprocated and exchanged." [3]

As a group, the fifteen women who were eventually selected (out of sixty-odd applicants) generally reflected the ethnic balance of MFY's client population: Seven were Spanish-speaking, six were Negroes, one was German-American, and one was an Italian-American. The only formal educational requirement was the ability to read and write English and to fill out simple forms and reports.

The homemaker staff was welcomed with much fanfare, including a tea attended by the director of the agency and other administrative staff. There ensued what can only be described as an elaborate courtship, including frequent encomiums, in envious tones,

[3] Gertrude Goldberg, "Untrained Neighborhood Workers in a Social Work Program," in Frank Riessman and Arthur Pearl, editors, *New Careers for the Poor* (New York, The Free Press of Glencoe, 1965), p. 139.

of the homemakers' lack of inhibition as compared to professional staff. Thus it was reported with some awe that one homemaker sucked lemons throughout a conference with the assistant director of the agency. "You're doin' fine, baby," said a homemaker to a psychiatrist at a staff party, "but twist a little harder!" The prevailing attitude was that indigenous personnel knew by virtue of their background what professionals did not or could not know or even feel.

Much of the comment on the homemakers' style had to do with how it differed from that of trained social workers, coupled with expressed delight in its effectiveness despite its disregard for established casework or psychiatric principles: "A homemaker with genuine contempt for a wretched housekeeper nevertheless helped her to improve her housekeeping. Rather than reacting negatively to the worker's judgmental attitude, the family responded warmly to her." [4] "The non-professionals are considerably less formal. They will hug clients, accept (and repay) their hospitality, and share first-name designations." "Non-professionals are unencumbered by 'professional role,' a concept that low-income clients rarely understand." The nonprofessional client relationship had more reality and more of the usual interaction between persons than is prescribed in the traditional professional relationship.[5]

Such observations introduced professionals who genuinely wanted to communicate with their clients to the problem of the distance they had to cover if they were to do it alone. "The discipline of the professional worker may seem colder or more rejecting to the client than the homemaker's direct, candid reaction even when it is harsh." [6] Apparently the hard-to-reach would not be so hard to reach if one could set aside the mystique of professionalism and concentrate on the task.

The homemakers maintained as their office a model four-room apartment in a local housing project. They did intake, escorted their clients to welfare and hospitals, gave out free samples on street corners of food they had prepared, and started countless

[4] George Brager, "The Indigenous Worker: A New Approach to the Social Work Technician," *Social Work*, Vol. 10, No. 2 (April 1965), p. 36.
[5] *Ibid.*, p. 37.
[6] *Ibid.*

dinners for clients returning late from appointments. During the first six months of service they handled approximately forty-eight cases intensively, only six of which failed to show improvement in home-management skills or in the use of community resources. However, about half of what was provided during this period was direct service, including child care. An average of eight preschool children a day were looked after in order that their mothers might shop, go to a clinic, look for an apartment, or the like. Some days there were fifteen children, two secretaries, ten to fifteen home-makers, thirty to forty clients, and too much confusion for one small four-room apartment—"an endless succession," as one woman described it, "of running noses and dirty diapers." Some-times mothers conveniently "forgot" their children until 8 P.M., and more than once a homemaker found herself with visiting children over the weekend.

The presenting reason for use of the Visiting Homemaker Service, whether it was for teaching, budgeting, shopping, etc., was usually related to the mother who was not entirely incompetent or incapable of taking care of things but simply overwhelmed by the multitude of tasks before her. The Visiting Homemakers Service was begun in December, 1962; during July and August of 1963, the homemakers cared for 299 children, ranging in age from two weeks to nine years. The clients themselves had identified what was most needed: Rather than have the neighbor lady's recipe for strawberry jam, they needed her to baby-sit for them. Services to Individuals and Families therefore turned to the development of the Visiting Homemakers Service as an experimental child-care operation, moving to larger quarters in the same housing project.

Some of the homemakers transferred to the new child-care service; others were assigned to work at the neighborhood service centers, where they could be immediately available for escort and translation. This new arrangement was part of the expansion and redefinition of neighborhood-service-center services. At that point in the history of Services to Individuals and Families came the realization that teaching a welfare client to make proper use of leftovers could not overcome the Department of Welfare's failure to provide her with a sufficient food allowance. The blame lay es-sentially with the institutions upon which her welfare depended, and this would have to be the first point of attack. So the home-makers, like all professional and nonprofessional workers in the neighborhood-service-centers, adopted the advocate role. Gradually most of the indigenous workers have come to carry case loads, a few as high as forty-five. They are assigned intake duties along with professional workers and now also share the title of social worker.

Nevertheless, by 1966 the romance was over. Sherman Barr, assistant chief of Services to Individuals and Families, stated that "those [of the visiting homemaker group] who were most effective had, in the main, experienced less poverty, were better educated, had managed their lives with a reasonable degree of success and productivity, and were also more sophisticated in making their way through various social agencies with which they had contact." [7] Indigenous workers were no longer valued for their indigenousness, their closeness to the client, or for sucking lemons or twisting hard, but for their ability to give service.

The object in the neighborhood service centers is the giving of service—direct, concrete service. Mr. Barr notes that "the ability to do more for the client was dependent in the final analysis not on the distinctive insights of a worker, professional or indigenous, but on the worker's . . . skill in providing immediate and relevant relief from stress, conflict, and deprivation." The purpose of a client's visit may be to get help in forcing her landlord to plaster the rat holes. If the worker does not succeed in pressuring him to do this, it hardly matters whether worker and client were able to relate to each other. Anyone who can get the landlord to do the plastering will be regarded as a good worker. According to Barr, people don't come to MFY to make friends or to establish an extended casework relationship (although the latter develops often enough because a lot of people have a lot of problems and keep coming back for additional help). Mostly they come because there are rat holes the landlord won't plaster or a mix-up with Welfare. In a service program it is the service that

[7] Sherman Barr, "Some Considerations in the Use of Sub-Professional and Indigenous Personnel," paper presented at the 44th National Conference of National Federation of Settlements and Neighborhood Centers, Chicago, May 26–28, 1966.

counts, and most people don't care who dispenses it as long as the help is genuine.

Because hopes were initially so high, the available reports on the use of indigenous personnel in the Services to Individuals and Families program suggest that the performance of nonprofessionals was more disappointing than it was in actuality. This has to do with the fact that the nature of the service itself was not understood at the outset, nor were the real needs of the target population known. Nor could the agency predict the results of its own experience. The interaction between indigenous and professional staff has resulted in the professionalization of the indigenous workers and in certain redefinitions of the professional role as well. "The indigenous staff's active direction, emphasis on external factors, physically oriented approach, partisanship, and pleas for action rather than talk were early major contributions to the development of a body of techniques for use by professional staff. Their importance cannot be underestimated." [8]

Furthermore, the indigenous personnel constantly applied a social rather than an intrapsychic definition of clients' problems. This was a significant contribution, for it provided a clue to how a client might view his problem and served as a corrective to rigidly psychological interpretations. Brager notes, "A homemaker touchingly ascribed the impulsive credit buying of a woman to the fact that 'being young, she wants everything in life'." When the same young woman reported a conversation with her dead husband, the homemaker acknowledged the woman's mental illness and recommended referral to a mental-hygiene clinic, although her further comment suggests that such diagnosis and referral might have been the result of supervisory influence: "My honest opinion is that she needs to remarry." [9] On the other hand, Charles Grosser states that "the longer a person occupies a subprofessional position, the more likely it is that his attitudes and values will shift in the direction of those held by professionals and thus away from the orientations of low-income residents. It casts some doubt

[8] *Ibid.*

[9] George A. Brager, "The Low-Income Nonprofessional," in Brager and Purcell, eds., *Community Action Against Poverty* (New Haven, College and University Press, 1967), pp. 169–70.

on the widely held assumption that the employment of nonprofessionals is a viable technique to bridge the cultural gap between professionals and the poor they serve." [10]

In talking with some of the original visiting homemakers who have been functioning as case aides for several years, it becomes clear that they have learned a good deal about social work. They are aware of much social-work method and process without having to use labels, and they can recognize the best professionals when they see them at work. They are also quite critical of the way in which many professionals handle cases. They regard themselves as valuable because certain people still confide things to them that would not be revealed to professional workers. Some feel that the kind of training which would enable them to acquire a degree of professional "distance" would permit them to function more efficiently. Others disagree, feeling that their efficiency is not impaired by extensive personal involvement.

A Department of Health, Education and Welfare report mentions, "If one takes people of ability and places them in a stimulating and demanding situation, it seems inevitable that they will expand the scope and content of their job and develop greater understanding and expertise in carrying it out." [11] For example, one former homemaker is currently instructing a class of teen-agers in shopping for and cooking American food. This project, sponsored by one of the welfare-action groups affiliated with the neighborhood service center, is in addition to her regular casework duties. Another ex-homemaker is now leading a sewing class. But these are, after all, only additional responsibilities which do not increase or raise job classifications for the indigenous worker.

One of the child-care workers is quoted as saying that she might long ago have directed the center had she only had "that little piece of paper to hang on the wall." The same report on neighborhood service centers says of indigenous workers that "their presence within centers will at the very least have had some effect on policies and practices and particularly on the other staff

[10] Grosser, op. cit.

[11] Robert Perlman and David Jones, Neighborhood Service Centers (Washington, D.C., U. S. Department of Health, Education and Welfare, 1967), p. 56.

with whom they have worked." [12] But after professionals acquire these techniques, after they have learned how to speak the language well enough to find their way around and are able to give the kind of service that is needed and wanted by their clients, what is to be done with or for those who have taught them? Do we tell the guide we no longer need his services because, among other things, he is not professional? Part of the problem of using indigenous personnel is that they have been thought of as aides or assistants. The MFY experience shows that some can function only in an aide capacity, if at all, while others are capable of considerably more. What makes the difference is, of course, the availability of training. It can be argued that the service will suffer while all these people are being trained. Such a situation could be avoided if money were available for training in agency budgets or if cities ran social-work training schools for the indigenous.

The most crucial consideration is whether there will be a place for trained indigenous personnel in the field of social welfare after Mobilization-type programs have run their course. Will there be neighborhood service centers run by settlement houses and private agencies that will hire the indigenous? Can the training provided by experimental agencies form a base for the worker's entrance into other agencies? It is hardly worthwhile to train people for work that is not going to be available tomorrow. And will social work as a profession be wiling to open its doors to the nonprofessional?

Essentially the issues over the use of nonprofessional personnel at Mobilization were raised as soon as Services to Individuals and Families set its priority as "the giving of concrete, immediate help to the poor" and defined the role of the social worker as an advocate for the client in his dealings with Welfare Department officials, landlords, school personnel, etc. The advocacy role, in its current level of practice and explication, does not require the practitioner to possess a master's degree in social work—any intelligent and articulate person, with common sense and organizational sophistication, can perform it reasonably well.

A number of interrelated factors pushed the indigenous personnel into this role. First, there were not enough professional

[12] *Ibid.*

social workers to meet the client demand for service; second, when the indigenous personnel functioned as homemakers, they were already doing a good deal of advocacy for their clients—for example, when they escorted clients to Welfare or helped them demand repairs from their landlords; third, many clients asked to see the indigenous personnel at the neighborhood service centers because they already had a relationship with them from the Visiting Homemaker Service or knew them from the neighborhood; and, finally, the indigenous workers wanted to do the job and have the status of social workers.

Although Barr is no doubt correct in saying that the more intelligent and sophisticated indigenous workers made better advocates, the question remains just how much intelligence, how much sophistication is necessary for effectiveness. There was consensus among professionally trained staff that if the agency could provide adequate training, indigenous personnel could take over professional jobs as they are now structured. The only proviso was that a neighborhood service center should be directed by a professionally trained worker, a pattern similar to group-work agencies in which the professionally trained group workers supervise the group leaders.

The argument has often been advanced that it is cheaper and more efficient to hire professionals to do the job than to set up a comprehensive training program, the results of which may be doubtful. The counter-argument is that there are important functions which indigenous personnel can perform better than professionals. Clients are often distrustful of professional workers and tend to withhold facts which they think would put them in disrepute. The amount of time required to break down this stereotype of the professional is generally not available in an operation where immediate service is necessary. Clients are less likely to react in this way to indigenous personnel. Second, the indigenous workers can help to spot professional romanticism. They are quick to point out that for some people the easy grant of money is self-defeating—no matter in what theoretical garb it is presented. Their life experience has taught them what clients perceive as legitimate and illegitimate demands from agencies. And finally, their actual physical presence in the neighborhood, evenings and weekends, at the same stores and on the same streets as the clients, increases the effective influence of the agency.

There is no clear answer to these issues. There is, however, a trend toward acceptance of the idea that in work with the poor, training is crucial, but that training need not be university training.[13] The indigenous personnel themselves classify the MFY clients into approximately three groups: One group needs only knowledge to help themselves; a second group needs knowledge and the support of a friendly agency, organization, or social worker; those in the third group cannot help themselves, either because of the sheer number of their accumulated concrete problems or because of disabling emotional problems. This is also the most adequate evaluation and description of how the indigenous workers themselves performed their jobs.[14] MFY's current efforts are geared to giving knowledge, support, and advocacy to clients. Indigenous workers are sure they can do the job—some say better than professionals. With training there is no doubt that a number of them can do quite well.

The fact was emphasized in early reports that indigenous personnel had difficulty facilitating communication "between the low-income resident and conventional persons and institutions: As persons of minority group status, without material or educational attainment, they are frequently dismissed by the personnel of the large service systems, barely accorded legitimacy in their official contacts with them." The homemakers reported that the very title "homemaker" barred the door. They found out quickly enough that phone calls to Welfare which began "This is Mrs. X, the homemaker from MFY" rarely had results, but if one said, "I

[13] A plan for training the indigenous for all levels of social-work practice can be found in Bertram M. Beck, "A Professional Approach to the Use of Nonprofessional Social Work Personnel," a paper presented at the American Psychiatric Association–National Association of Social Workers Conference on Nonprofessionals, Washington, D.C., May 1967.

[14] This was the opinion of the professional staff. See Ann Graziano, "Services to Individuals and Families' Staff Recruited from the Low-Income Community" (mimeographed, New York, MFY, September 1967), pp. 3–4. ". . . the term 'indigenous worker' is more descriptive of the geographical location of a worker than of the presence of common traits or characteristics. In other words, we reject the proposition that all, or even the majority of workers, fall into a common mold."

am Mrs. X from MFY," or "I am a social worker from MFY," the conversation could continue. "Homemaker" is, after all, only a fancy word for housekeeper, which is, after all, a maid. "I could go to Fourteenth Street anytime and pick up day work if I wanted that," reported one woman. Having done much more, they want the recognition that is due them, and they insist that opportunities in general be made more available for indigenous workers within the agency.

5

From Reform School to Society

Hettie Jones

Among the major concerns in a program intended to prevent juvenile delinquency are youngsters who have already committed crimes—those who have served a term in a correctional institution and are ready to return to society. MFY's Reintegration Project proposed to deal with some of the approximately one hundred youthful offenders who return to the Lower East Side each year from various correctional institutions. The object of the program was to prevent recidivism—that is, the commission of another offense which would require recommitment. The rate of juvenile recidivism in the MFY area in 1962 was estimated to be as high as 80 percent.

A number of theories have been offered to explain why these rates are so high, why a youngster who has committed a crime for which he has been imprisoned tends to repeat the same behavior, requiring additional punishment, reform, treatment, or training—all of which mean the removal of the child from his home and his isolation from society. The assumption on which the Reintegration Project (RP) was based is that the high rates of recidivism are due not simply to the correctional institution's failure to rehabilitate the offender but to the fact that persons and institutions in the community to which he returns have erected barriers to his becoming an acceptable citizen. The released offender comes back to his old haunts, to the same influences which contributed to his initial lawbreaking, except that now he has the additional burden of being an ex-inmate, regarded as a potentially bad influence on everyone else. Schools are reluctant to accept him; a job, even a menial one, is hard to find; his family may try to restrict his activities; the parents of his friends may not wish them to associate with him. These restrictions of opportunities for conformity appear to prevent him from leading a law-abiding life; he recidivates even though he may have been motivated to make good during his stay in the institution. It was the intent of the Reintegration Project to eliminate barriers to conformity so that the young people in the program would no longer have to repeat the same round of illegal activities.[1] Opportunities were to be extended to released offenders, as to other youth in the neighborhood, through available resources in the community as well as through MFY's own work and education programs.

According to the Proposal, the Reintegration Unit (RU) was to be informed by the courts and other agencies when any young offender from the area was formally committed to an institution. Cases would be chosen from among those who were to be sent away for the first time to a New York State training school and would include some defined by the RU as difficult. Contact would be made as soon after commitment as possible and was to continue until the client's readjustment was assured or his failure definitely established (by his return to an institution or his becoming known to a higher court through further delinquent behavior).

Once a youth was accepted in the program, a case record was to be compiled with special attention paid to his school, work, and leisure-time behavior, and his family relationships. On the basis of this record and subsequent reports from the institution, the RU worker, with the youngster and his family, would develop a plan for his reintegration. Decisions were to be made regarding the desirability of further school versus work, the type of schooling or training best suited to his needs, where the client should live after release (if his home was deemed not the best place), and ways

---

[1] The program assumed that the way in which ex-offenders are defined determines the way in which people respond to them. Thus a dual barrier to be removed was the way people and institutions defined and acted toward returned inmates.

in which he might be helped to associate with "conforming peers and adults" instead of his old friends when he returned.

The worker assigned to the case would be responsible for carrying through the plan. In addition, he was to intervene with appropriate persons in schools, employment resources, and the community in an attempt to enlist their aid on his client's behalf. In turn, the youth was to be trained by his worker to make use of any opportunities provided. Constant contact with the client would keep the worker informed of any difficulties he encountered at school, on the job, or in the community at large.

Since recidivism is not fully understood, it was also expected that research conducted along with the action program would provide valuable data for the study of this problem, relevant also to other slum areas. For research purposes, MFY planned to make detailed observations based on daily contact with one hundred young offenders. Systematic interviews were also to be conducted with youngsters and adults significant in the clients' lives. By gathering this information MFY hoped to learn more about the experiences of released offenders as they affected reintegration into the community and recidivism.

Beginning in September 1962, arrangements were made for the release of a certain number of youth directly in the care of MFY, which promised to report regularly on their progress to the Home Service Bureau, the after-care (or parole) division of the N.Y. State Training Schools. The program was started with nineteen cases distributed among various state institutions. Initially the plan was to work with some youths who had been committed to public institutions as well as with all those who had been committed to private institutions from the MFY area. However, this plan would have required a larger staff than was called for in the original Proposal. When a decision was reached assigning each worker a caseload of no more than fifteen, the Reintegration Unit was automatically limited in size.

Just at the time the program was launched, the New York State Family Court Reorganization Act was passed. This act substantially reduced the number of youngsters available for the project by establishing that a child judged a "person in need of supervision" might under no circumstances be committed to an institution. Only those judged to be delinquent—that is, those who had committed acts which would be considered crimes if done by adults—could henceforth be committed. The act also guaranteed law guardians for all minors. As a result, many cases which formerly went directly to the court were now more carefully screened for out-of-court adjustment.

Because of the restrictions imposed by the new act, the number of cases available for research was limited. The study population totaled fifty-eight youths, thirty-four of whom were serviced by the RU and regarded as experimental, and twenty-four of whom were serviced by the Home Service Bureau and regarded as a control group.[2] No girls were included in the research sample

TABLE I

	Total (58)		Experimental (34)		Control (24)	
	No.	Per-cent	No.	Per-cent	No.	Per-cent
Age at Interview						
14–16	14	24.1	10	29.4	4	16.7
17 and over	44	75.9	24	70.6	20	88.3
Ethnicity						
Puerto Rican	30	51.7	15	44.2	15	62.5
Negro	16	27.6	13	28.2	3	12.5
White	12	20.7	6	17.6	6	25.0
Religion						
Roman Catholic	39	67.2	21	61.8	18	75.0
Protestant	18	31.1	13	38.2	5	20.8
Other	1	1.7	—	—	1	4.2
Reason for First Committal						
Theft, burglary	19	32.8	15	44.1	4	16.7
Truancy, maladjustment at school	17	29.3	6	17.6	11	45.8
Maladjustment at home	8	13.8	4	11.8	4	16.7
Fighting, assault	8	13.8	5	14.7	3	12.5
Other	6	10.3	4	11.8	2	8.3

[2] This population comprised those served during the last year of the project's operation, 1965–66.

since there were too few available for the study; however, a small
number were serviced by the Reintegration Unit. Table I presents
data on the age, ethnicity, religion, and offense of both experimental and control groups.

According to arrangements made with the training schools,
youths who were to be paroled to MFY were contacted mostly at
Youth House (the N.Y.C. detention point) prior to their commitment to a school. Workers visited clients once a month during
their stay in the institution. Families were contacted at the point
of commitment and were encouraged to visit their children.

The Family

Involvement with the families of the target population substantially increased the number of persons, all with problems requiring consideration and time, for whom the Unit became virtually
responsible. The families of the first twenty-eight youths paroled
to the Reintegration Unit in 1963 consisted of forty-seven adults
and ninety-four other children, which meant 169 human beings
to be serviced, not just the twenty-eight assigned to the project.
Forty-three percent of those families were receiving public assistance and required help with food, housing, and health problems,
and sometimes direct financial assistance when emergencies arose.
The average family was involved with at least four social agencies
—typically public assistance, health services, public housing, and
various community-center services. (One family had been known to
sixteen agencies in the area.) A report issued in July 1963 notes
that plans for the optimal treatment of these families specified that
an average of five additional services would have to be provided.[3]
Even with the small case load each worker carried, evening and
weekend work was commonplace.

Merely arranging for parents to visit children in institutions
took time and effort: If a family is on public assistance, traveling
expenses must be granted by the Department of Welfare after a
letter from the Home Service Bureau. Approval of such a grant

[3] Robert Ontell and Wyatt Jones, "Discontinuities in the Social Treatment of Juvenile Offenders" (mimeographed, New York, Mobilization For
Youth, 1964).

takes a while, and according to the RU supervisor, the amounts granted were generally not enough. (The Department of Welfare provides one fare only.) Although families were not encouraged to depend on MFY, the burden of arranging for continued contact between parents and children in the program fell on the reintegration workers. Maintaining relationships between people who are separated is in itself no easy task. Many of the adults were illiterate or nearly so; others were unwilling to write letters. The difficulty of traveling long distances (especially if one cannot speak or read English) is very real. Letters to the reintegration workers from youths in the training schools often begged for news of home, friends, family members who hadn't written. "Have you seen my mother, I haven't heard from her." "Tell Benjamin I said hello and ask him if he received my letter." "Tell my mother I said hi to her and I'll be seeing her soon."

A number of youngsters who came under the care of the Reintegration Project were from intact homes, with both parents present; some of them also had siblings who were law-abiding. In other intact homes, one or more of the siblings had come to the attention of the courts. Most of these youngsters were paroled to their families, with MFY supplying casework services to all family members and additional supportive services to the youth. But in cases where there had been family conflict prior to a boy's removal from home, even attempts at intensive family casework failed to remove it or alleviate it except for a time. Returning an adolescent offender to a Lower East Side family in conflict is something like returning a wounded soldier to the front.

There is no doubt that the location of the Reintegration Project (like all of MFY) in the neighborhood and its availabilty to both the youths and their families did much to keep them involved and motivate them to use the service. (One youngster still in the training school wrote to his worker that he was glad she knew what the neighborhood was like.) But getting a multiproblem Lower East Side family on its feet was not always possible, especially since the institutions designed to help them often confounded their predicament. And a family's intact appearance was frequently found to be a mere facade.

The Reintegration Unit's involvement with the families of clients was included in the original Proposal as part of the master plan for each client's reintegration. But, as in other areas of the Services to Individuals and Families program having to do with multi-problem families, MFY had not anticipated how far any family service would have to go in order to take real care of the needs the clients presented. Nor was it fully aware of the limitations various bureaucracies imposed on their clients' lives. The small staff of the RU—involved in endless procedures to comply with or cut through the red tape, trying to maintain connections between the clients and their families even after the boys had returned—was simply overloaded. However, they could not overlook the family problems, especially since they found family breakdown so frequently contributing to the delinquency of their clients.

The problem was not generally that the parents were disinterested in the welfare of their child. The families participating in this study many times gave evidence of a genuine desire to help the child out of his difficulties and prevent a repetition.

The children themselves declared that when their truancy or minor lawbreaking became known to their parents, they were usually punished in some manner, enough to stop them for a time. Yet eventually they drifted back into trouble. Many defied their parents by disappearing completely or, as the court petitions declare, becoming beyond control. To a parent on the Lower East Side who is familiar with what the street has to offer in the way of major conflict with the law, bringing a minor to the attention of the court while there is still some chance is not necessarily a way of relinquishing responsibility. "Before he gets in real trouble" is the usual description.

The ordinary strain between generations also applies to these families, but it is complicated by such matters as culture conflicts and the opposition of rural and urban values, which help to destroy traditional family structures and attitudes. It is not uncommon to find a mother who knows no English at all trying desperately to communicate with a teen-age son who does not express himself very well in Spanish, perhaps because he is unwilling to do so, perhaps because his whole world outside his home has urged him to become part of the dominant culture. This is a classic immigrant problem and will disappear in time, but the problem is no less real because it has happened before. Intervention to interpret one world to another may alleviate some of the stress.

In February 1964 the Reintegration Unit formed a mothers' group which met once a month to exchange ideas on community problems as well as problems related to their institutionalized children. Sometimes members brought along friends or neighbors in similar situations. To judge from the size of the group (from three to sixteen participants), and from the animation exhibited in the discussions, only those highly motivated attended. But attendance was voluntary; after a few months of spotty turnouts the group was discontinued. There were just too many more pressing things for workers and parents to do. A clearer focus about what the goals of the group were and some form of required attendance were clearly needed.

The alternative to attempts to reintegrate the youth into his former environment is foster placement. In some instances this is adjudged necessary by the courts; in others the child is asked to choose. This is a difficult decision to ask of an adolescent: What youngster, even knowing that foster placement might be a good idea, is willing to relinquish his blood ties—no matter how diseased—for another, possibly risky situation? If the record reads that Robert is "quite ambivalent toward his parents" and therefore fails to follow through on the placement arrangements he has expressly requested, can it be said that this child has failed to help himself to a new life? Can he be offered guarantees that whatever he gets into will be better than what he had? One child, after much discussion, opted for foster placement and then disappeared just before he was to embark on his new life.

Employment

It was after the first ten youths assigned to the project returned from the training schools that workers began to feel that the help they could offer in areas other than family casework was limited. If a youth was over sixteen and chose not to return to school, he could be referred for employment, but a referral does not necessarily mean a job. Priority arrangements established with MFY's World of Work provided some definite placements, but few of the

RU youngsters were able to stay with that program. The reasons given were that the employment provided had too little meaning or personal involvement for them. The Reintegration Project youth became frustrated more easily, demanded more of the counselors, and became discouraged sooner. Although some were highly successful, the majority remained unskilled and unemployed despite training. One such client refused to accept any jobs at $50 or $65 per week when he could make $75 easily by "hustling." He was discharged from the program when he reached eighteen because "there was nothing else MFY could do for him."

Countless appointments for job interviews were made which the youngsters did not keep. One boy, talking with his worker about the possibility of a work assignment, mentioned that he had lost his Social Security card. He was advised to get another, but his record does not show whether he accomplished this on his own. A worker noted: "He became a trifle bitter because he was unable to secure employment, but he was appreciative of our efforts to help him and superficially has verbalized his understanding of the limitations of our resources." Upon his release another boy took a newspaper delivery job that entailed his getting up at 5 A.M. and consequently slept through most of his classes. But his parents could not afford to give him any pocket money, and he did want to go to school. In some cases even involving a boy in a job where he functioned well did little good. One boy took a job in a flower shop, but after a few weeks the owner—for reasons known only to himself—declared that he needed the youngster only a few hours a week, if that. Another youngster, employed in the MFY luncheonette, was regarded as "a very good worker, amiable and very well liked by others," but was arrested two weeks later, accused of stabbing an old man to death.

But the most relevant fact is that for most of these boys, as well as for their law-abiding counterparts, the possibility of getting and holding a job that means anything at all is very slim. In the first place, they are qualified to do very little. Secondly, their work habits are poor. Thirdly, their aspirations were often unrealistic.[4]

[4] See the chapter on "An Appraisal of Youth Employment Programs" in Vol. 3, *Employment and Educational Services*, for a discussion of how these problems can be overcome.

And if a boy has repeatedly stated that he wants to be a navigator, in spite of his inability to read or to do mathematics beyond a fourth-grade level, it is going to be difficult to persuade him to push a handtruck in the garment district. One of the questions put to the reintegration clients by research was "Do you think you'll ever get to be what you want to be?" The boy who wanted to be a navigator was aware of his educational limitations and mentioned that he'd probably end up working in a factory. By the time a boy is over sixteen and has already been in trouble, he may have given up planning and hoping, but he is still child enough to dream. The connection between dreams and the reality of accomplishment must be made early. Crash programs, such as those of MFY's Employment Division, were generally unable in such a short time to make connections that had been lacking for so long. Many of the reintegration clients could not adapt to the working world, which requires regular attendance, punctuality, and a certain amount of diligence even of a delivery boy. Perhaps this is because the delivery boy knows, other things being equal, that he will never be other than a delivery boy, never be the boy of his dreams.

It is interesting to compare what is expected in the way of dedication from a sixteen-year-old boy of limited background from a deprived family and what is expected from a middle-class, fairly well-educated youth. The middle-class teen-ager in America is required to be diligent in his schoolwork in the interest of future rewards, but his lapses are passed off as youthful spirits, and he is generally given much freedom to postpone arranging his own life. Responsibility, when it is assigned, is more in the nature of keeping the lawn trimmed than earning money to pay part of the rent.

On the other hand, the sixteen-year-old high-school dropout is not only required to decide, right here and now, exactly what he will be, but to do it with a minimum of "trouble." He is urged to be sober and serious, to work during the day at a job which usually involves some physical labor and then, if possible, to continue his schooling at night. We require of him the kind of motivation traditionally required of immigrants and their children, yet we make no promises that he will attain the stature of those who spend these years going to school and football games, even if he behaves as we wish him to. This is a hard role for a sixteen year old. The young black and Puerto Rican man of limited advantage knows full well that he stands hardly a chance of ever getting anywhere, especially since so few of the significant adults in his life ever have. The youth of the Lower East Side sometimes choose hustling for very real reasons.

The School Experience

For those who chose to return to school there was a different kind of ordeal. Boys who before had been unable to accept the school as it was presented to them, who had been unwilling to accept the standards given as relevant to them, and who had persistenly truanted—some as far back as kindergarten—now returned to school at a disadvantage. A child cannot automatically reenter the school system in New York City after a term at an institution; there are papers to be processed through the Board of Education, and this means a waiting period. For high-school students the time is about a month, for 600 (behavior-problem) schools and CRMD (remedial) classes, the wait is at least two months, even when there is pressure to have a student reenrolled.

An ex-inmate is usually not returned to the same school he was attending before his conviction. The Reintegration Project's experience in this area did not differ from that of the Home Service Bureau; it took four months to place one child in a 600 school, and during that time he again became involved in antisocial activities. Another youngster reading at a third-grade level was promised a junior-high-school diploma if he maintained perfect attendance; he tried to, but he was so lost in the classroom that he just couldn't continue. A third was assigned to a 600 school and after some improvement was transferred to a junior high school. His misbehavior there landed him back in the 600 school but, angered and frustrated and obviously capable of doing more than the 600 school required, on graduation day he let the air out of the tires of visiting officials' cars.

A specialized high school to which one girl requested entrance wrote, "Even though the mother and the girl insist on registration at this school, the placement must still be made through the Board of High School Placement, and only on condition that we are willing to accept the student." In addition, the course she asked for was overcrowded; if accepted (after admissions tests), the girl would have had to apply for other courses in which she was much less interested. The outcome was her placement in a regular high school where she immediately established a pattern of truancy and later quit. In some cases school placement, or part of the procedure, was left up to the parents, and further complications ensued: "Mr. S. failed to take Louis to school appointments. Louis was getting anxious. Finally, worker took him."

The vocational high schools in New York are overcrowded, and placement generally is made only with pressure. Two MFY workers accompanied five boys to a 9 A.M. appointment with a Board of Education placement official. The official, who arrived at 11:15, assured them that there were no openings available at vocational schools and that in addition the boys had to go through one term of regular high school before they could be considered. However, one boy whose record was particularly impressive was granted an interview at the vocational school, after considerable MFY effort.

Like a stuck phonograph, the Reintegration Project records reveal the same patterns of disorder and deficiency, but the main theme is truancy. What turns up in nearly all reports is the school's failure to be meaningful for the child, and the child's increasing unwillingness to attend at all. Often the workers escorted their clients to school for a few days to start them off, but most of the children stopped going as soon as they were left on their own.

"One of the most glaring problems for Steven is his inability to read and its consequences." The same Steven reports that he was unhappy not being in school and that would "force him to turn to stealing and drinking." His mother maintained that he was a bright boy and that the 600 school to which he was sent completely demoralized him. In 1960, at the age of nine, Steven had a verbal IQ of 108. By November 1964, when he came to the attention of the authorities for the third time and was sent to a training school, his verbal IQ was 80. After he had been in the school for two months, it was down to 67. The crime that resulted in his finally being sent away was his theft, with two other boys, of two shirts from a department store. No doubt he should have been in school at the time. The 600 schools of the New York City school system, in which the emphasis is on attendance and conduct rather than achievement, are regarded by those who have attended them as a waste of time. Every Reintegration Project youngster has reported: "They don't teach us anything there. Why should I go just to sit around?"

During the second year of the project a remedial reading and arithmetic program was begun. Two teachers, with additional tutors, were used four days a week from 3:30 to 5 P.M. in a local community center. But only a small number of those in the project could be persuaded to participate, and these were the very young of the target population. The older ones were too self-conscious about their lack of skills; it was also hard for them to be in school all day without knowing what went on and then be asked to experiment with another set of learning procedures after 3:30. Nevertheless, the remedial program was maintained until the summer of 1965, when funds were finally discontinued, though by this time it serviced mostly the younger siblings of boys in the Reintegration Project, and thus became for all practical purposes a preventive rather than a cure.

Conclusions

The Reintegration Unit made little headway in altering the policies of social agencies. Sometimes the conflicting interests of the various agencies concerned with one child or family operated directly against the interests of the client. In one case, this was the outcome of the joint efforts of a settlement house, the RU, and other agencies: "Nothing was done to help this child. The agencies involved were too concerned with not hurting one another and in not antagonizing the parents."

For those Reintegration Project youths who did get into further trouble help and advice were available from MFY's Legal Services Unit.[5] The courts themselves were receptive to MFY ideas

5 See especially Vol. 4, *Justice and the Law.*

regarding future planning for these youngsters, but the choice of what to do with them was extremely limited. Either they were returned to an institution—and MFY sometimes had to recommend this—or they were not. There was no program of limited control available, such as a community-based halfway house, where the youngster could be presented with as much community participation as he could handle. But in any case, these youngsters would have to be considered recidivists for their connection with the Reintegration Project did not prevent their reengagement in illegal and antisocial activity. MFY sometimes opted for recommitment, because the harsh truth was that at the institution the youngster at least had a place to sleep, some measure of care, and of course supervision.

One of the problems that confronted the Reintegration Project was that it could not look after its clients constantly. The daily contact projected in the Proposal was never possible, and consequently most of what constituted the lives of the youngsters in this study went unnoticed until crises arose. And by that time, it was almost invariably too late to do anything but return the client to an institution or release him from the project.

> . . . a call from Mrs. B., Juan's stepmother, was received informing us that Juan is involved with a gang on Clinton Street and that he's in trouble with the police. She would not give any further details. Juan has been living with her . . . instead of his father . . . for the past month or so. He has been staying away from home, and she does not know his current whereabouts. His father is currently in jail. Recently Juan has been working, but it lasted only for a week. She complained that Juan was uncontrollable and desperately wanted our help to contain him. Before realizing that this was an MFY case, I gave her an appointment at the office . . . [for two days later], which she did not keep.

Perhaps the most relevant question is why Juan's whereabouts were unknown to both his stepmother and his worker. It is very easy to get lost in a slum if one wishes to do so. In such a situation all the worker can do is attempt to reach his client. If the client refused to be reached, failed to keep appointments or respond to letters, the Reintegration Project was able to do little. Those who cooperated were served. "A. is seventeen years old and is reluctant to receive casework services from MFY. As he no longer wishes our help . . ." Unfortunately, whether he wished casework service or not, A. was unable to hold a job for more than a short time and could have used further assistance. But no specific methods were developed for capturing the imagination or even the presence of these youngsters, especially of the more malcontent among them.

The Reintegration Project came up against the same institutional barriers which had been recognized in the preliminary research which led to the mounting of the program, and it was unable, finally, to arrive at specific methods for pushing them aside. The Project, through its involvement in caring for the eighty-nine families in its charge during its four-year history, became an intensive family casework unit. After some youngsters were returned to training schools or dismissed from the program because of additional brushes with the law, their families continued to be serviced, since there were siblings for whom preventive service was considered important.[6] The Reintegration Project did not lower the rate of recidivism, nor did it test the theory of opportunity on

TABLE II

	Total (58)		Experimental (34)		Control (24)	
	No.	Percent	No.	Percent	No.	Percent
Placed in Opportunity Systems	57	98.3	34	100.0	23	95.8
School only	18	31.1	12	35.3	6	25.0
Work only	10	17.2	4	11.8	6	25.0
Both	29	50.0	18	52.9	11	45.8
Not Placed in Opportunity System	1	1.7	—	—	1	4.2

[6] One observer commented that the workers did not know how to change the way local institutions defined and acted toward ex-inmates and therefore did what they were most comfortable with, family casework.

which it supposedly was based. The following statistics compiled by the research division will serve to clarify these conclusions.

This table shows that youngsters in both the experimental and control groups (serviced by the Home Service Bureau only) had access to legitimate opportunity structures. Only one was not placed in either system, whereas about half in both groups found access to both systems.

One of the stated functions of the Reintegration Unit workers was not only to have a client gain access to an opportunity system but to provide the support and guidance that would keep him in it or enable him to make a transition from one system to another with a minimum of conflict. The following information is relevant:

TABLE III

	Total (58)		Experi-mental (34)		Control (24)	
	No.	Per-cent	No.	Per-cent	No.	Per-cent
Stayed in Opportunity System	31	53.5	19	55.9	12	50.0
School only	9	15.6	6	17.6	3	12.5
Work only	4	6.9	2	5.9	2	8.3
Both	18	31.0	11	31.4	7	29.2
Dropped Out of Opportunity System	26	44.8	15	44.1	11	45.8
School only	9	15.5	6	17.6	3	12.4
Work only	6	10.3	2	5.9	4	16.7
Both	11	19.0	7	20.6	4	16.7
Not Placed in Opportunity System	1	1.7	—	—	1	4.2

This table shows that the Reintegration Project was not significantly more effective in keeping youngsters in the opportunity system, once access was gained, than the Home Service Bureau.

Did the service provided by the Reintegration Project have any effect in reducing the rate of recidivism?

TABLE IV

	Total (58)		Experi-mental (34)		Control (24)		Home Service Bureau* (1,151)	
	No.	Per-cent	No.	Per-cent	No.	Per-cent	No.	Per-cent
Nonrecidivists	34	58.6	20	58.8	14	58.3	666	57.9
Recidivists	24	41.4	14	41.2	10	41.7	485	42.1

* These figures come from the Tenth Annual Home Service Bureau Report and include the experimental and control populations 4/1/65–3/31/66.

This table shows that there were no differences in the rates of recidivism for the experimental and control groups.

Did staying in an opportunity system have any effect on the rate of recidivism?

TABLE V

	Total (58)		Stay in System (31)		Drop from System (26)		Not in System (1)	
	No.	Per-cent	No.	Per-cent	No.	Per-cent	No.	Per-cent
Nonrecidivists	34	58.6	16	51.6	18	69.2	—	—
Recidivists	24	41.4	15	48.4	8	30.8	1	100.0

Although the sample is too small to permit reliable conclusions, Table V seems to show that staying in some opportunity system had no significant relationship with recidivism. In fact, a larger percentage of the dropouts were in the nonrecidivist group.

At the close of the study, seventy-five youngsters from the MFY area who had been released from a training school at least a year earlier were supposed to comprise the sample for the above statistics. Forty-three of these were part of the experimental group and thirty-two were part of the control group. It is of some significance that, of these seventy-five, only fifty-eight could be located. Seventeen boys had disappeared.

What, if any, are the alternatives to the Reintegration Project? As it was conducted, it differed from the Home Service Bureau only in case loads, which were smaller. The Project was supposed to test the theory of opportunity by removing community barriers to conformity. But what barriers were destroyed? The statistics show that every child save one gained access to an opportunity system (either work or school). Everything, finally, depended on the child himself. If he wished to resist casework approaches, he could do so; if he wished to truant and hang out, he might; if he wished to disappear entirely, he was even able to do that. The missing factor is authority—authority that would not be of the variety provided by families already confused, pressured, and intimidated, or by social workers, who could only urge. A halfway house has been mentioned as one method. Adolescents require limits to their world, which may be gradually enlarged as they become more capable of functioning as adults. This is especially true of children coming directly from the closed, structured world of a training school. If you are fathoms deep, you must come up slowly; otherwise you get the bends.

Since under present conditions it is impossible to release a youngster into the slum from which he came and expect him automatically to avoid his previous pattern of life, then a very clear pattern must be constructed for him. Authority is necessary to accomplish this, an authority which can make its influence stronger and more attractive than that presented by the street. Such an authority might be helped by group support. Think of the respectability of Alcoholics Anonymous or the help provided by Synanon. A recidivist is also an addict of sorts, hooked on truancy and crime and perpetual requests for control. The most clever are those who can support their habits without getting caught.

Finally there is some question regarding the entire process. Is it advisable to remove a child so completely from his environment and then throw him back into it with inadequate preparation, having made no real change in the environment itself? In a rural training school, away from all the lure and pleasure of the city, one does not learn to deal with the coming reality. It might be worthwhile to attempt a more continuous process instead of such abrupt leaps and training more in line with the life that will face the youngster when he is on his own.

The same holds for family adjustment. If retraining consists partly in a boy's learning to live in a peer-group environment, how is he to learn to live with his parents and siblings? The societal order of the training schools comes very close to the boy's experience with his friends on the outside, except that relatively few opportunities exist for destructive behavior. A boy in a training school is responsible to his peers as well as to authority, but it must be remembered that this is a group of delinquent peers. It may be that one can learn to recognize freedom only when it is denied, but denial does not teach one how to use freedom carefully, as must be the case when one functions in a free environment.

With reference to community attitudes toward released offenders—the invidious definitions and barriers to conformity—much has still to be done. Negative attitudes toward them make possible the bureaucratic indifference, the inadequate training schools, and the uncontrolled slum environment. The juvenile offender is a bad boy today, as always.

It was the opinion of the director of the project that "we have come too late in the lives of these children." It is true that they have been stunted and warped by the slum: "Down where I live at you can't help but get in trouble." Nearly every experience they report is stressful. They stick together, they love their families but are ambivalent about whether their families are too strict, they are sorry to be in trouble and won't get in trouble again, they spend hardly any time at home and their parents don't know where they are, they need control over their behavior but really don't belong in training school, they hate cops and the police pick on them. But these are only reports of their behavior, of which they are ashamed and about which they lie a good deal too. They seem seldom to have been asked or challenged: "What shall we do with you? What is it about your world that should be changed?" Such a straightforward approach by the helping professions might be more in line with reality.

Their attitudes toward therapeutic people, at best noncommittal, stem partly from the conviction that no one is going to offer them anything but a very difficult struggle with no guaranteed rewards, and also from their knowledge that they can slip easily from one world to another, that they can "put on" authority and appear quite sincere without being so. "If you play it smooth, you'll get out early. You do what you're told, you'll get out; if you're hard-headed, you may never get out." When an attempt was made six months after the close of the Reintegration Project to interview some former clients, only one response was received, and that from the mother of a boy who had managed to get into the army. One boy in a training school suggested: "You saying a lot of words and making a lot of motions, but when you bring it all up to-gether, you ain't said nothing." The object is to *say*—and this means *do* or *communicate*—something.

The Reintegration Project has shown the need for changes in the policies and procedures of social agencies, a restructuring of training schools to conform to the demands of urban life, and a benevolent but firm authority in the lives of released offenders, as well as the need to involve them in their own reintegration. It has also shown that, although the task is overwhelming and the expense enormous, prevention of delinquency must be the first order of business. Otherwise we may find ourselves tomorrow experimenting with the children of today's subjects.

6

Psychological Help for the Poor

Hettie Jones and Harold H. Weissman

Freud has been quoted as saying, "We shall probably discover that the poor are even less ready to part with their neuroses than the rich, because the life that awaits them when they recover has no attraction." [1] The attempts of Services to Individuals and Families have been directed toward making the lives of the poor more attractive, at least in terms of the physical and material aspects which are their due under the law.

The decision to limit neighborhood-service-center activities to concrete service, as noted in a previous paper, was not based on a belief that poor people have no need for psychological help. Then, as now, it was known that the poor have more mental illness than is found elsewhere in the population, as well as "normal neuroses" and all the psychological problems that stem from poverty. But it was also known that one cannot easily talk about psychological difficulties to a man overwhelmed by material and social problems.

The neighborhood-service-center experience sheds considerable light on the reasons behind the well-documented tendency of private social agencies to refrain from offering their psychological services to the poor.[2] An enormous amount of staff time was required to deal with the varied social and emotional difficulties of

[1] As quoted in Robert Coles, "Journey into the Mind of the Lower Depths," *New Republic,* (February 15, 1964).
[2] See the chapter on "Overview of Services to Individuals and Families" in this volume, n. 4.

the so-called multiproblem family. That public agencies, such as housing authorities, schools, and welfare departments, rarely work effectively for poor families is well-known. The technique of treating the situational and emotional problems of clients is vague.[3]

In this context, at the neighborhood service centers Mobilization opted for helping clients with their situational problems, implicitly at least, because such help was thought to be the best means of engaging the clients in a therapeutic process and of understanding their needs. In so doing it became clear that there are a number of kinds of psychological help as well as a number of ways of giving this help. As Dr. Robert Coles has remarked, "The problem is that of understanding the world the poor and the outcast inhabit, the world of their lives and feelings, and equally of understanding what our attitudes toward them are, what our world is willing and unwilling to do for them." [4] MFY has been concerned with developing this understanding.

Psychological Insight on Self and Systems

Initially there were three experimental programs in addition to the neighborhod service centers which provided psychological services as part of their overall service to clients: the Reintegration

[3] Mary Williams suggests another reason. "The caseworker in SIF [Services to Individuals and Families] . . . nurtured on Freud and, increasingly, the ego psychiatrists, must employ the bulk of his . . . training in . . . study-diagnosis, not necessarily treatment or action. . . . I have some question about the dictum that study-diagnosis and treatment are parts of the same process. . . . I believe that the caseworker may study and diagnose and not treat a given client. I grant that the element of generalized support, prevalant throughout these two processes, may make the treatment to follow less threatening. . . . The result of the study-diagnosis complication seems to me to be demonstrated by the fact that many of us can offer a wealth of information and deep insights about our clients, individually and collectively, but we are befuddled about how this information is fashioned into a treatment program which will (1) not alienate our clients and (2) have some impact on their personality or behavior. Our traditional training leaves us ill equipped to . . . initiate and progressively execute a treatment program when we may be debating what in our storehouse of knowledge is to be used and even how we are to evaluate success." "Detailed Notes of a Professional Social Worker in a Mobilization for Youth Neighborhood Service Center," (mimeographed, New York, Mobilization For Youth, 1965).

[4] Coles, op. cit.

Project (treated in detail in another paper), the School-Community Relations Program, and the Internal Services Unit (ISU). Also under Services to Individuals and Families administration were special programs operated at two local mental-hygiene clinics under contract to MFY which were available for referrals.

The Internal Services Unit was a short-lived (about eight months) attempt to offer casework support for youngsters involved in other MFY programs, mainly the work programs. Boys with problems serious enough to limit their participation—for example, a trainee with such bad acne that he would not go to job interviews—were referred to the ISU for guidance and counseling. The unit was terminated after eight months of operation because its staff—two professional workers and a supervisor—were urgently needed in the neighborhod service centers where caseloads were rapidly increasing.

The School-Community Relations Program was transferred to Services to Individuals and Families from the Division of Educational Opportunities in 1963. It sought to minimize the social distance between middle-class school and lower-class family in order to obtain the cooperation of both in encouraging a child's education. Each worker was assigned to a school in the area. Children having school difficulties were referred to the worker who, along with teachers and the assistant principal (usually the one in charge of behavior), would attempt some treatment relative to both school and home. It was inevitably found that the multiproblem family was also multiperson. Workers in this program had case loads of eight to twelve only, but each "case" involved from two to ten people in addition to the troubled youngster. The concrete problems of each family were described by one worker as monumental. Yet, starting from some very basic beginnings—for example, uniting a mother and children who had been living apart, getting an apartment where they might live, dealing with the Department of Welfare—and progressing from such concrete service to regular appointments at the home or in school, workers were able to persuade many parents to join the PTA, form relationships with their children's teachers, and explore the effects of their own behavior on the home-school adjustment of their children. Service included advocacy, legal advice in consultation with MFY's Legal

Services Unit (helping a client to file suit or fight a dispossess),
setting up hospital appointments, getting the Department of Welfare to provide full instead of partial support, filling out housing
applications—all under the heading of helping to make a connection between home and school.

The other side of the coin included attempts to reveal to
teachers—through home visits, workshops, and conferences—
something of the lives of the children they taught. For Kenny's
teacher even to begin to understand his behavior it was vital that
she visit the three-room walk-up on "Junkie Corner" where he
and his mother and six other children lived on welfare. She came
back with nothing but praise for a mother who could get seven
youngsters to school "on time every day and dressed so neatly"
in the conditions in which the family lived.

All this work with teachers and family, with school officials
and lawyers, the Department of Welfare, after-school programs,
hospitals, and other concerned agencies was sometimes necessary
to prevent the school suspension of one child in trouble. Aside
from any consideration of therapy, the psychological support provided to the children in this program was incalculable. But so were
the time and effort required to make any breakthrough.

In terms of casework techniques, the School-Community Relations Program offered few methodological innovations. In dealing with Negro and Puerto Rican clients, social attitudes—particularly hostility and methods of coping with it—were generally
discussed openly, with the result that clients were brought to a
new level of awareness regarding their own as well as white people's positions on civil rights and other issues. Most worker-client
meetings took place in the home or in informal community settings
rather than in offices. The use of the worker as interpreter or
liaison with the school system also constituted an innovation. The
worker functioned not only to refit the troubled child into the setting but also to get the setting—and this meant mostly the teacher
—to adapt to the child. Thus Kenny's teacher, for example, was
encouraged to include in her curriculum Puerto Rican Discovery
Day and the civil rights sit-in demonstrations and reportedly was
"amazed at how knowledgeable the kids were in areas that mattered to them."

Although the social workers for the most part accomplished what they set out to do—begin to bridge the gap between school and home and redirect the troubled youngster so that he could function effectively in both worlds—there were, of course, difficulties. These were more often related to the inflexibility of the school system, the inability or unwillingness of school officials—teachers, guidance counselors, principals, etc.—to make needed adaptations, than to lack of cooperation by the families concerned. The program was discontinued in June 1966, since it had been funded only as a four-year experiment.

Such programs as the School-Community Relations Program illustrate what is involved in applying traditional casework, in work with multiproblem, multiperson, low-income families. It is apparent that, with sufficient time and effort, low-income clients can be moved through the complexities of their situations and toward some understanding of themselves as well as their position in the larger society. Clients can be helped to function in a system such as the school system, and successful functioning is itself a considerable source of psychological help, for a number of reasons: It demonstrates that the person can move in at least one area or system without disrupting the rest of his life; the system itself often rewards participants for successful functioning, and what has been learned about functioning in one system may carry over into others. However, if any significant progress is to be made, efforts to improve clients' functioning must be coupled with institutional change.

Social Involvement as Psychological Help

One of MFY's original goals was to alter self-defeating patterns of behavior through the provision of opportunities. It has been suggested that these opportunities will not be adequately used unless the psychological impediments attached to poverty are removed.

Not all the poor are mentally ill according to the commonly accepted definition, but *most* poor people are caught in a pattern of hopelessness. Their inability to break out creates a disposition toward emotional illness. Even if one were to provide overnight all the accoutrements of affluence—money, housing, schools, health facilities, etc.—the problem of generational (as opposed to situational) poverty would still exist. There would be some people who were unable to utilize these opportunities at all.

It is important to develop opportunities in sensitive relation to the perception by the poor of their own needs. When this is not done, the poor are not likely to be able to use efficiently the opportunities created for them. Rather than to provide opportunities for the "lower class," the poor must as a group be helped to secure opportunities for themselves. Only then will motivation be released that is now locked in the silent and usually successful battle of the neighborhoods of poverty to maintain themselves as an alien social world. This motivation . . . will enable them to enter the majority society and make it as nurturant of them as it is at present of the more prosperous population.[5]

This is not to suggest that advocacy on behalf of the poor should be suddenly abolished and all efforts concentrated on altering self-defeating behavior. That would be tantamount to a refusal to apply a tourniquet until the patient's blood type can be determined. Furthermore, it is clear that the systems that serve the poor are partly responsible for reinforcing their self-destructive patterns of behavior.

Dr. Haggstrom has noted that the poor, to counteract their sense of powerlessness, draw upon other sources of power—family and religious groups, for example, and even the neighborhood service center. Lending power to the poor through the NSC advocacy service is a beginning, but it is still a loan. Dr. Haggstrom adds that the self-conception of the poor is not always the same as our social definition of them. They resist attempts to make of their life such a meagre thing, and it is this resistance that "makes it possible to attempt the otherwise herculean task of . . . helping the poor themselves . . . to become strong and effective enough to challenge the invidious definitions that have been made of them." [6]

[5] Warren C. Haggstrom, "The Power of the Poor," in Frank Riessman, Jerome Cohen, and Arthur Pearl, editors, *Mental Health of the Poor: New Treatment Approaches for Low-Income People* (New York, The Free Press of Glencoe, 1964), pp. 219–20.

[6] *Ibid.*, p. 218.

In late 1965 the first of the welfare-action groups was organized by a trained community-organization worker attached to a neighborhood service center. The group, composed mainly of women who were clients of the center, was organized around the issue of bringing everyone up to the minimum standard of subsistence set by the Department of Welfare. There are now many such groups throughout the country. One New York group alone in the summer of 1966 obtained $50,000 for its members in its minimum-standards campaign. Subgroups within the large groups have been formed for home study and problem sharing; there are sewing classes and English classes and a group studying American cooking.

The women have picketed the Department of Welfare and negotiated with the commissioner around certain issues. They have sat in at various Department of Welfare offices. These activities have not gone unnoticed in the mass media. Although focused on institutional change, they have also produced changes in individuals—from dressing better to enrolling in a training program and getting a job.

Forming groups around the welfare issue is one of several innovative techniques to give people's lives back into their own keeping, to renew their autonomy—a necessary development for psychological growth. And the welfare groups are already a much more effective source of pressure for change in the Department of Welfare than all of MFY's advocacy.

It is probably difficult for people accustomed to more traditional clinical models to see the welfare organizations as therapeutic. Nevertheless, at University Settlement psychiatrists have referred clients to these organizations. Their view is that there are many methods of psychological help beyond the office-based interview, including the placement of clients in groups organized for the purpose of institutional change.

Clinic Referral

Although workers at Mobilization's neighborhood service centers have been specifically directed not to give long-term psychological help, clients frequently come in to talk about their problems. A woman comes to the NSC because someone has tried to break into her apartment, and she wants to be reassured that she can get over her fright without having to pick up everything and move away. Clients ask for advice about family matters. A young woman feels guilty and despondent over finding herself pregnant. Workers, of course, meet such situations and psychological crises as best they can, but unless a person is having severe difficulties which the worker feels warrant referral to a mental-hygiene clinic, no additional arrangements or psychological diagnoses are made.[7]

Mobilization has had contracts with two mental-hygiene clinics in the area—Henry Street and University Settlement—since 1963. At each clinic two workers function as an experimental unit, the purpose of which is to test traditional casework treatment with lower-class clients and to experiment with newer methods, such as family-centered treatment. The director of Services to Individuals and Families worked closely with these units to ensure both their experimental nature and their coordination with the neighborhood service centers.

Although there was some difficulty at first, mostly in locating proper personnel for the job, both clinics have found this arrangement satisfactory. Service has focused on finding new and more effective methods to reach the severely afflicted. The clinics have found their contact with MFY neighborhood service centers, job-training programs, and legal services to be of considerable value in treating their clients.

In reporting on the program, University Settlement recommended continued and intensified contact by clinic personnel with groups of teachers, guidance counselors, religious leaders, etc. Such contact maintained on a regular basis often leads to better understanding by all concerned and coordinated planning for these families. Some children, if the whole family situation is known, can be helped by schoolteachers or similar contacts and may not need the help of a mental-hygiene clinic.

[7] Many workers left the agency after the first year of neighborhood-service-center operation because they wished to practice traditional casework and were simply overwhelmed by the number and type of problems that clients brought. Time wasn't available to do long-term counseling.

The report from the Henry Street clinic is directly relevant to any consideration of giving help in the form of psychological insight to the poor, partly because it describes a breakthrough in the type and availability of service offered and partly because it comments on the main problem of divorcing concrete from psychological help:

The established pattern of administration of services by social agencies and clinics, determined by specializations in function . . . results in fragmentation of service to individuals and families, and the necessity for a family to be simultaneously under care of a multiplicity of agencies if all their needs are to be met. In limiting its function to brief concrete services, MFY conformed to this pattern, and . . . in effect separated the emotional-psychological aspects of problems from the concrete, whereas the clinic, once it undertook to serve an individual and/or family, used the holistic approach from its view that all problems are interrelated.[8] The consquences of fragmentation were evident at the point of referral to the clinic, in the families' reaction to the break in the continuity of help they were getting from MFY. . . . Clinic staff has gone beyond its normally aggressive efforts to reach and involve these families in taking service, and even with this expenditure in time and energy our efforts were unsuccessful in some of the cases. . . . The meaningfulness of this kind of situation to families whose experience with agency help has been one of being buffeted and rejected should not be discounted as an improtant factor in judgments of "resistance" to their taking help.

Directly related to this comment is the question of who is to be referred to a psychiatric clinic—what kinds of problems are, after all, the province of which agency. The report notes:

Of the 98 individuals who have gone into treatment, 13 needed and received psychotherapy by a psychiatrist, two drug-therapy supervision, and 83 casework counseling services with the family as the focus. These figures obviously raise the question as to the soundness of using a psychiatric facility for the treatment of social-emotional problems which are inherent in a family breakdown, and

[8] It should be borne in mind that the yearly caseload of this clinic was about equal to the weekly caseload of a neighborhood service center.

problems which family casework agencies regard as appropriate for their services. In other words, the fact that a psychiatric problem is detected in a member of the family does not always mean that a psychiatric intervention is either necessary or the best method of attack. Our experience would indicate that casework and other services of a concrete nature, family centered, are most needed by and are most useful to the populations both agencies serve.

The importance of this experience cannot be overemphasized. For what is diagnosed as mental illness among the poor is often the result of their interaction with an environment which treats them as the poor—and that means treats them poorly. To insist on continued separation of services would be to persist in the long-outmoded idea that one's mental, physical, personal, and social life are not intertwined.

Henry Street's method of service was in many ways an innovation, as shown in its report:

> The clinic abolished the practice of a "waiting list" five years ago and has nevertheless continued to meet the demand for its services without concomitant increase in personnel by implementing the fundamental principle that not all people need or can use the same form of treatment in the same way. Specifically, the clinic has for a long time been providing brief, short-term, crisis, emergency, walk-in, periodic and long-term treatment, all within this concept. Its staff has provided this range of service in the clinic and in the homes of families. It has . . . also diversified its methods . . . from individual therapy to group, joint counseling of parents to family-focused treatment, as well as drug therapy—in short, adapting its knowledge and skills to fit what any individual patient or family can best use. Above all, the clinic has directed its efforts to a unity as well as a continuity of service to an individual and family.

Psychiatrists at Henry Street have begun to look at the whole person and his environment instead of only at sickness. They have begun to consider how psychiatric symptoms are related to the life of the community, to unemployment, war, prejudice, and anonymity, poor schools, and slums. Dr. Coles notes that "when the community is ignored as not very relevant to symptoms, lives are described in terms which either fail to account for much that happens to people or else deny the continuity, unpredictability, and ambiguity of human experience." [9] He cites schools which teach students about "vitamin deficiencies, parasitic infestation, or the diseases that rats carry, without the slightest interest in fastening those discussions to human beings living not very far away from the schools." [10] The same observation applies to the curricula of social-work schools, where the idea of giving psychological help is not applied to situations outside the office interview.[11]

Conclusion

In terms of offering psychological help to the poor, the single most important idea developed through Services to Individuals and Families has been the importance of concrete services. Mary Williams comments as follows:

> Concrete services . . . suggest to me a way in which the social-work profession may begin to break into the deprived person's view of us as "magical . . . unfeeling . . . preachy." I would define concrete services simply as any substantive act on the part of the practitioner which is readily discernible to the client, ideally proposed by the client, and having about it the potential for immediate relief from stress. I would see it as employing action in behalf of the client rather than instruction or information given to the client so that he might act in his own behalf. I subscribe to concrete service because I believe it "start (s) where the client is," gives the social worker a means of diagnosing the deprived (who recoil from history-taking), counteracts their sense of hopelessness and distrust, relieves stress and demonstrates good will. . . . Unfortunately, we sometimes place too much stress on concrete service . . . when, in essence, it is only the beginning for a significant proportion of our clients. . . . It is in regard to the significant proportion that my re-

9 Coles, *op. cit.*
10 *Ibid.*
11 A mobile service center has been suggested for the Lower East Side in an innovative means of offering help in cases of emotional breakdown. At present, when such cases are brought to anyone's attention, it is only to that of the police. It is clear that some social agency must assume responsibility for informing the community that it is ready to serve those with severe emotional problems. The presence of large numbers of such persons in slum neighborhoods exacerbates the areas' problems.

marks are addressed. . . . I believe the concrete service has a temporary, limited, palliative effect, making the person "feel good" but not clearly suggesting to them the need to review the B-H-H (Blameless-Hopeless-Helpless) syndrome, a symptom of defeat and despair which is so blatantly compounded in their daily lives. Let us remember that we are with our clients one or two hours a week, we are not the world to them. . . . Further, encapsulated concrete services are not going to change that world. What we are talking about, after all, is the use of concrete services to change the clients' *view* of their world so that they might more productively engage it. Are we not then talking about some, however limited, form of behavorial change or educative process? . . . I think so, and for that reason view concrete services as the . . . essential, irreversible step to be used planfully along an ongoing continuum. They are, however, also present in every phase of the continuum.[12]

In establishing its neighborhood-service-center policy to concentrate on clients' material well-being, the agency has been mindful of the argument that it is crucial to treat the whole client, to see all of his problems in perspective, and to go beyond the mere giving of concrete service. Without disputing this argument, MFY has simply affirmed that it lacks the resources to operationalize a whole-client treatment approach, and that in many cases such an approach cannot succeed in the *aggregate* unless change can be induced in service systems, such as the Department of Welfare, and unless the poverty which produces a variety of emotional problems for people can be reduced.[13]

Of perhaps equal significance to ideas about concrete services has been the development at Services to Individuals and Families of conceptions about the different kinds of psychological help:

. . . aiding someone with an immediate problem by giving concrete assistance like money or legal aid can be a form of psychological

[12] Williams, *op. cit.*

[13] It should be borne in mind that Mobilization sought to serve the economically lowest 20 percent of the population. This segment is the most dependent on public agencies. There is no doubt that many clients could benefit from a process such as described above by Mary Williams. The question is one of priority based on availability of resources, the life situation of clients, which part of the population is to be served, and conceptions about the nature of individual and social change.

help; making it possible for a client to function in a particular system is another; involving a client in social action related to meeting his needs is a third; and providing a client with insight into his motivation and actions is a fourth.

Nevertheless, Services to Individuals and Families did not differentially apply these techniques. The agency chose not to look at its clients from the point of view of how to help them psychologically to cope with their situation; it chose, rather, to see to it that their situation was first a tolerable one. Given the fact that the life situation of most of the clients was at best extremely difficult, this policy was justified, if for no other reason than to see what results it would produce.

Group Services

PART II

Group Services

7

Overview of Group Services

Beverly Luther

In the late 1950's, the Lower East Side of New York had become a battleground for teen-age gangs. Teen-agers were invading the settlement houses rather than entering them; they were attacking one another after dances; they were refusing to participate in activities with members of other ethnic groups; they were militantly denying members of rival gangs access to their turf, whether that was defined as a street, a settlement house, or a school playground. Everyone was concerned: the police, the Youth Board, local merchants and residents, the schools, and especially the youth-serving agencies.

In the Mobilization area, serving approximately 43,000 youths under the age of twenty, there were eleven large social settlements or recreational agencies, a like number of recreational programs under church sponsorship, a system of after-school recreation at local schools conducted by the Board of Education, and an extensive park system and public-recreation program. Compared to other slums this was one of the best-serviced areas in the United States, both in quantity and quality. There were more professionally trained group workers per thousand teen-agers in the Mobilization area than in any other area of comparable size in the country. The outbreak of youthful violence clearly implied that some change in method or program was needed in the agencies.

Since their beginnings in the early twentieth century, the settlement houses had maintained a youth-serving emphasis. This focus had given rise to a variety of programs: physical fitness and athletic activties, health and medical programs, arts and crafts, clubs and informal associations, mental-hygiene clinics, etc. Each of these programs embodied some idea or theory about child growth and development. Thus psychological theories underlay the mental-hygiene clinic, educational and cultural theories inspired the dramatics and arts emphasis, new views on medicine led to the health programs and so on.[1]

After World War II the settlements turned increasingly to group work as developed by social workers for their major operating body of knowledge. This field emphasizes the potential for individual growth and development through group experiences guided by a trained group worker. Yet the field of group work, while united in the belief that individuals can be influenced through group activities, was quite disunited as to how groups could best be used in the prevention or cure of delinquency. Some emphasized a form of group therapy, others had a task or work orientation similar to the CCC concept, others emphasized the effect on delinquents of the group experience in devolping and carrying through programs, and still others saw the group as a means of establishing meaningful relationships with individual members. No single emphasis dominated any of the settlements, but each point of view had its adherents.

It was not possible in 1960, when the Mobilization Proposal was written, to marshal data to prove or disprove any of the current programmatic cures for delinquency. It was clear, though, that the existing group-work techniques were not well grounded in a theory of the development, prevention, and cure of delinquency. As has been noted, Mobilization's Proposal took the opportunity theory of Cloward and Ohlin as its major theoretical underpinning. Instead of using the group as its central programmatic mechanism, the project was geared toward social systems and providing opportunities for individuals within these systems:

> . . . it is our belief that much delinquent behavior is engendered because opportunities for conformity are limited. . . . The essence

[1] For a discussion of the progam in settlements, see Harold H. Weissman and Henry Heifetz, "The Changing Program Emphases of Settlement Houses," *Social Work* (October 1968).

of our approach to prevention, rehabilitation, and social control in the field of juvenile delinquency may be stated as follows: In order to reduce the incidence of delinquent behavior or to rehabilitate persons who are already enmeshed in delinquent patterns, we must provide the social and psychological resources that make conformity possible. Rehabilitation, for example, cannot be achieved simply by encouraging the offender to want to conform. . . . If the possibilities for a conventional adjustment are restricted or absent, the likelihood is that the offender, no matter how favorably motivated, will continue to engage in non-conforming behavior. Thus we must concern ourselves with expanding opportunities for conventional behavior.[2]

To Cloward and Ohlin, "opportunities" included jobs, education, and a variety of social and medical services. Group and recreational services were important only in the sense that such programs were often the only contact the conventional world seemed to have with the older delinquents. This view was antithetical to the ideas of some settlement-house leaders, who felt that their particular programs were valid and that all they needed were the money and staff to carry them out on a larger scale. This policy dilemma was never formally resolved; instead, a compromise was struck: Contracts would be written with the various settlement houses for a variety of group programs. These programs, the Detached Worker, Preadolescent and Adventure Corps programs, would also serve as recruiting agencies for other programs and services within Mobilization. In addition, Mobilization itself would mount three experimental programs involving group services: the coffee shops, the Group Abstinence Program for addicts, and the Young Adult Action Group.

The Preadolescent Program was intended to discourage younger children from imitating the behavior of teen-age gang members by offering attractive alternatives. The plan was to employ skilled group workers in teams, based in community agencies, to resocialize predelinquents so that they could eventually be moved into regular community-center programs. The life styles and needs of preadolescent lower-class youth were to be emphasized, and

[2] *A Proposal for the Prevention and Control of Delinquency by Expanding Opportunities* (New York, Mobilization For Youth, 1961), p. 45.

special tutoring and educational efforts offered. Local teen-agers who were successful in school and in social relations in general would be hired as assistants to the group workers. Parents would be encouraged to help with the groups and also to form their own parent associations.

The Detached Worker Program was to make use of all the vocational and school resources offered by Mobilization. The workers were to go out on the streets and meet the gangs in order to become a social bridge between gang members and school authorities, potential employers, the courts, the police, etc. Thus the detached worker, in addition to his attempts to control conflict behavior and establish close relationships with gang members, was to be the channel between street gangs and the major institutions of the community.

The Adventure Corps was designed specifically for potentially delinquent boys and girls aged nine to thirteen. A primary objective was to develop a lower-class youth culture which could compete succssfully with the delinquent subculture. To accomplish this task the Adventure Corps was to introduce programs that gave recognition to such expressive qualities of lower-class youth as "heart," as well as provide adventure, discipline, and action within a formal, paramilitary structure, complete with ranks and rewards.

The Group Abstinence Program was an experiment to determine whether a group of drug addicts could be rehabilitated through an ordered, sequential set of group and individual activities. The group was first to be detoxified, then given work training and group-living experiences outside their home community, then returned to their home environment for individual work training while living together as a group, and finally reintegrated into their home and family environment.

The Young Adult Action Group was designed to test the hypothesis that delinquent and delinquency-prone teen-agers could become involved in social action and social-protest activities, and that this involvement would serve as a viable substitute for delinquent activities and as a means of helping the youth to develop ties with conventional society.

The coffee-shops project envisioned three storefront cultural centers, each having the appearance of a coffee shop. The project was designed to provide a recreational and cultural experience for low-income youth, aged sixteen to twenty-one, that would serve as an alternative to various deviant forms of recreation. It was hoped that the coffee shops would become neutral turf, where members of rival gangs could meet without conflict. Each coffee shop would have a distinctive artistic or cultural motif: an art center, devoted to Negro and Puerto Rican art and culture; a folk-jazz center; and a gallery for display of local artists' work. The project by its nature was to emphasize creation rather than conflict in an adolescent's life; the focus would be on the cooperative building and maintenance of a social facility. Natural leaders of the various gangs were to be formed into a managerial group to control and plan operations. By taking on legitimate prestigious roles, it was hoped that these youngsters would demonstrate constructive leadership for the youth members. Finally, the coffee shops were to offer special resources for training youngsters with talent and interest in various cultural and artistic areas, as well as serve as a center for individual counseling and assistance.

The papers in this section analyze the results achieved in these various group-service programs and attempt to determine the extent to which various theoretical ideas concerning group work and delinquency were supported or disproved. The prevailing ideology at Mobilization in 1962 was that recreation and group work as practiced at local social settlements was unrelated to the real needs of the delinquent or would-be delinquent. The excitement in the early days of Mobilization was in other areas of programming. For this reason, none of the group-services programs was subjected to formal research, and the programs tended to operate independently. In addition, the Preadolescent and Detached Worker programs were carried out with different program emphases and techniques in different settlements. Mobilization did not and often could not insist on uniform operational procedures. These factors complicate an analysis of the group-services programs.

Notwithstanding the low priority given to group services, a great deal of experimentation and modification took place to meet emergent problems. Entirely new program concepts, such as an Adolescent Service Center, were developed, and older ones such as the coffee shops were adapted into a Cultural Arts Program. By

1967 Mobilization's attitude and theoretical orientation toward recreation were begining to change dramatically. Instead of seeing work and play as separate, as was the tendency in 1962, the agency was engaged in developing programs which related recreation and play to work and education. The reasons for this shift will be apparent in the papers that follow.[3]

[3] The yearly budgets for the department were as follows: 1962–63, $309, 712; 1963–64, $525,755; 1964–65, $549,553; 1965–66, $579,764; 1966–67. $596,036. The figures do not include indirect costs for fiscal services, executive offices, public information, central services, personnel department, and occupancy costs. Indirect costs averaged 25 percent per year. The National Institute of Mental Health and the Office of Juvenile Delinquency were the major funding sources for the program.

8

Group Service Programs and Their Effect on Delinquents

Beverly Luther

The intellectual origins of Mobilization's group-service programs can be traced to Frederick Thrasher's sociological classic, *The Gang*. In this book, written some thirty years ago, Thrasher described the criminal behavior of a number of delinquent gangs in Chicago. He concluded that delinquency could be attacked successfully only through a systematic, community-wide approach, encompassing all phases of the predelinquent experience. This would include analysis of all children to find those most likely to become delinquent and a deliberate use of institutional supports and programs in their behalf. Since potential delinquents, as Thrasher noted, are especially prevalent in blighted, declining, and interstitial areas of cities, he recommended that action be concentrated in these areas. On recreational facilities in particular he wrote:

> The common assumption that the problem of delinquency will be solved by the multiplication of playgrounds and social centers in gang areas is entirely erroneous. The physical layout of gangland provides a realm of adventure with which no playground can compete. The lack is not of this sort. The real problem is one of developing in these areas or introducing into them leaders who can organize the play of boys, direct it into wholesome channels and

give it social significance. Ganging is merely one symptom of deepening community disorganization.[1]

In this study Thrasher was not specifically concerned with how play could be used to prevent or treat delinquency. Rather, he tried to describe the part that recreation and play, among other factors, have in the total life experience of the gang. Drawing on the work of Thrasher and of Albert Cohen, whose book *Delinquent Boys*[2] emphasized the crucial role of the peer group, Cloward and Ohlin added a new element:

> The tendency of social workers is to explore the motivations underlying the individual's membership in a delinquent group, to assess the ways in which he has learned to satisfy his needs through antisocial behavior. The result, whether intended or not, is often to explain the existence of the gang on the basis of the maladjustment of its individual members, without acknowledging the influence of the social order. The projected remedies are thus of an exclusively individual nature, and the ideological and structural foundations of the social order are unchallenged.[3]

The MFY Group Services Department, based on the Cloward-Ohlin theories, was concerned with affecting the structural arrangements of society which were believed to foster gangs and delinquency, and the individual lives of gang members. This paper will review the effects of four programs aimed particularly at the problems of delinquents: the Detached Worker, Preadolescent, Adventure Corps, and Coffee Shop programs.

The Detached Worker Program

A detached worker is a social worker who goes out into the streets and other meeting places of gangs to offer his services.

[1] Frederick M. Thrasher, *The Gang: A Study of 1,313 Gangs in Chicago* (Chicago, University of Chicago Press, 1936), p. 494.

[2] Albert K. Cohen, *Delinquent Boys, The Culture of the Gang* (Glencoe, Illinois, The Free Press, 1965).

[3] *A Proposal for the Prevention and Control of Delinquency by Expanding Opportunities* (New York, Mobilization For Youth, 1961), p. 71.

This often results in a long-term relationship between gang and worker, and usually requires that the worker spend a great deal of time with the gang in their neighborhood haunts. The worker allocates most of his time to on-the-street relationship-building contacts with gang members. This permits immediate intervention in the emergencies that regularly confront groups or their individual members. Their often irrational responses to these crises, along with their lack of knowledge of other potential responses, commit gang youths even more deeply to deviant behavior. It has been noted, however, that where a meaningful personal relationship exists, youngsters will seek the worker's help even when the worker is physically absent—telephoning, visiting the agency, leaving a message with other gang members, etc.

The MFY Detached Worker program had the advantage of being able to draw upon several years' experience with similar programs in New York and other parts of the country. The results of these programs were mixed:

> Detached-worker programs undoubtedly reduce conflict behavior, at least while the worker is assigned to the group. The intervention of a trusted adult who advises caution, settles disputes, and provides face-saving alternatives generally results in a diminution of conflict. Increased status as tough guys is gained by members of gangs to which a worker is assigned, and this too may lessen the need for "bopping." However, the long-range effectiveness of such programs may be questioned . . . only negligible differences have been found between gangs and control groups in the frequency of members' involvement in criminal and socially disapproved behavior. This was so although there was little question regarding the competence of workers, the good relationships established, and the effectiveness of the project in increasing participation in organized recreation.[4]

The Detached Worker Program at MFY shared the traditional concern with redirecting the gang's energies and interests into socially acceptable leisure time pursuits as well as establishing close personal relationships between the workers and individual

---

[4] Walter B. Miller, "Brief Summary of Impact Findings of the Roxbury Youth Project" (mimeographed, 1961).

gang members.[5] But the MFY program had a new emphasis as
well: The worker was to be a social broker. It was his job to increase the gang members' awareness and use of services and programs of the community and MFY, especially vocational and
educational services. Earlier detached-worker programs had placed
much greater emphasis on recreational services.

During each of the four years of its existence, the Detached
Worker Program reached from fifteen to twenty gangs. According to a report by one of the workers, these boys had resisted
previous attempts to encourage sustained contact with any specific
agency-sponsored recreational program:

> Many of these gang groups, with a history of expulsion from
> settlement-house programs, do not easily accept the rules of the
> agency. . . . The weightiness of the gang member's social reality—
> extremely poor educational background, use of addicting drugs,
> sexual deviance and promiscuity, unemployment, and even for
> some a daily search for food—supports his perception of the set-
> tlement house as a place for children.

Above all else, the boys exhibited overwhelming feelings of in-
adequacy, fear, and ignorance; at the same time, many of them
also had such positive qualities as generosity, intelligence, and
strength. Many of them verbalized the desire to break completely
away from the gang, but, retarded socially and emotionally, they
continued to seek each other out during leisure hours. Marijuana
and alcohol were often used to give them the necessary courage
to move out.

The vocational and educational problems the boys had were
no less profound than their social problems. That there was a
need for an adult with whom these youth can feel some rapport,
whom they can regard as interested in them, cannot be doubted.
Boys who have been described as vicious hoodlums reacted in the
following way when their worker was about to leave them:

[5] The local settlements and the New York City Youth Board were under contract to MFY to run detached-worker programs. These agencies
hired and supervised their own staff. In addition, during the first year of
its operation, MFY ran a small detached-worker program in an area not
then served by any other agency.

Nobody brought up the subject of my leaving until we had almost reached the Lower East Side. Then, to my surprise, Leo started it, asking why did I have to leave. Victor chimed in saying that he had never known anyone like me before. I said that I was glad that I had been able to show them that there were people different from many they had known.

I stopped . . . to let Rick and Tony out. As soon as I stopped, Hank jumped up, grabbed my arm, kissed it twice, saying real fast, "Good-bye Wilkins," and ran up the street. This struck Victor and Pedro as funny, and they howled with laughter. I did not laugh, because this was quite moving to me. Rick had a suspicion of a tear as he said quite soberly with extended hand, "Good-bye, Wilkins, and thank you for all the help you have given me."

The detached worker performed a variety of tasks for the gang, from organizing camping trips to intervening with the courts and providing jobs. For the older adolescents who wanted to move out on their own into the job world and into adult relationships, the worker was able to make effective use of MFY's employment and educational services. Yet the patterns of some of the boys did not change quickly. Alcohol, drugs, lack of self-confidence, lack of job skills, and educational deficits reinforce each other and make long-term support necessary. With younger adolescents, the group and the group recreational program tended to be more important.

The risk for a detached worker, as for any service giver who wants to affect the behavior of recipients of his service, is that the client will accept help, such as legal assistance, but not alter his deviant activities. This risk must be taken, especially in slums. Programs such as the Detached Worker Program are best evaluated in terms of levels of goals. The fact that higher goals are unattainable does not necessarily mean that a program should be discarded; the attainable lower-level goal may be quite valuable. When an adolescent's whole environment supports deviant adaptations, a cadre of detached workers, no matter how skilled or strong of personality, cannot alone cure delinquency by harnessing peer support for socially acceptable adaptations. They can, however, by serving as a link to society's institutions, provide help for individual delinquents with their personal problems in school, court, etc., and this is a valuable contribution.

Attempts were made to bridge the gap between gang youth and the major social institutions that define their life chances; some measure of success has been achieved. Workers have influenced court actions by drawing on the resources of the agency's legal unit and by developing alternatives to incarceration acceptable to the courts. Home visits by workers have reduced the stress experienced by already overburdened, debilitated family units that are always tempted to apathy as an alternate solution to seemingly insoluble and relentless problems. Work opportunities made available through the agency's youth-employment program measurably enhance the worker's ability to persuade gang youths to adopt more conforming behavior. Representation at police precincts has encouraged a more thoughtful use of the discretionary powers of police officials at the crucial moments of arrest and arraignment.

In giving help and designing programs, it must be remembered that delinquents, like any other group of adolescents, differ among themselves.[6] No one program or facility can succeed with all of them. Recognizing this fact, in 1966 the settlements involved in MFY's Detached Worker Program opened up several storefront adolescent service centers and also began a community-organization effort to interest local adults in dealing with the problem of delinquency.[7]

The Preadolescent Program

The Preadolescent Program, operated under contract by local settlement houses, established groups of delinquent-prone youngsters, aged eight to twelve. Its basic purpose was to interrupt delinquent patterns and resocialize the youngsters so that they could eventually participate in regular community-center programs. This was to be done by using a team approach with a staff of pro-

[6] It is as difficult to define "the" cause of delinquency as it is to cure it. Some delinquency is certainly situational in origin, some is psychological, some structural or sociological, or perhaps some combination of these. A variety of cures are therefore needed.

[7] See the chapter on "Adolescent Service Centers" in this volume.

fessional group workers assisted by local teen-agers who were succeeding in high school. Program content was to reflect lower-class interests and styles. Parents of the children were to help in leadership of the groups and were to be included in family-life education classes.

Each year the program served approximately four hundred children in the area, in twenty-five to thirty groups. Some children were referred by truant officers, others who came to the settlements were sent because of their disruptive behavior there, some were recruited directly off the streets. Very few of the agencies utilized local teen leadership, and none developed any strikingly innovative programs. However, time was made available for staff to get to know the parents of each child as well as to involve themselves in the child's problems in school, in court, and at home. In addition, agency facilities were available more often to group members, due to the greater availability of staff provided by the program. Preadolescent groups of this kind, left to their own devices, had tended to disrupt agency programs. Increased specialized staff made it possible to contain them within the bounds of the agency.

A typical group met once a week for two hours at the center. Every third week, an all-day session was added. In addition, the group participated together with other groups in the center in the Friday movie and Saturday gym programs.

The opportunity for staff to devote considerable time to these groups had an important consequence. At first the staff workers tended to use a traditional approach, attempting to involve pre-adolescents in programs as the main mechanism of potential change. Later, the emphasis was on involving the youngsters in a program so that the worker could become acquainted with the individual problems—problems which could not be resolved through the group program. The program thus became a means through which staff workers developed relationships with the preadolescents.

Each of the contracting agencies tended to emphasize different aspects of the program. There was little coordination among the participating settlements. Some of these agencies viewed Mobilization as lax in this respect, while Mobilization staff charged the agencies with resisting change. Notwithstanding the lack of co-ordination, certain conclusions can be drawn from the program. The following is an excerpt from an evaluation done by one of the workers:

> First, the program was able neither to retard nor reverse or pre-vent delinquency in children from multiproblem families who were al-ready confirmed in antisocial patterns. The general effect of the program was that contact with the courts allowed for earlier place-ment in a foster home or institution than may have been possible if the children were unsupervised by any agency. This early place-ment in itself may be a positive value in the prevention of later adult delinquency.
>
> Second, whether or not the program was able to prevent delin-quency, it was nevertheless effective in establishing contact with families of problem children and at times securing help for helping them to make contact with other agencies and services, especially the schools. It seems wise to recruit younger brothers for groups in order to maintain or continue contact with certain families.
>
> Third, indigenous leadership can have negative as well as posi-tive effects. When the leadership comes from a teen-ager who is himself confirmed in a pattern of delinquent behavior, he may help to provide group control within the agency, but be a negative factor on the group in the community.
>
> Finally, the major problem encountered with all groups in dif-fering degrees was disruptive behavior. While it was possible to over-come this problem, there was nevertheless . . . a tendency for the group worker to be diverted from his more therapeutic goals to put most of his effort into control problems.
>
> It should be noted that work with families where the parents speak only Spanish can be effective only when the worker knows that language; otherwise it remains a constant barrier to com-munication and understanding.

As this evaluation suggests, it was clear by the end of the 1965–66 program year that the Preadolescent Program had accom-plished very little with groups of boys who had a well-established gang pattern.[8] The program was considerably more successful

[8] One worker speculated that the agency, by focusing on group pro-grams, was merely strengthening the group, so that outside the agency it was better able than ever to engage in concerted delinquent activity.

with groups less confirmed in delinquent patterns. With the confirmed delinquent groups, the Preadolescent Program might have been more effective had it sought to use the group program to break down the groups' cohesiveness. This would have been difficult to accomplish, for it is clear that settlements, although giving lip service to the idea that some groups should be broken up, actually evaluate their workers on their ability to maintain groups within agency limits. Very seldom did these agencies move consciously and systematically in the direction of breaking up groups.

For the 1966–67 program year, utilizing the Pread staff, an experiment was undertaken, based on the hypothesis that the single best indicator of predelinquency is truancy and a general inability to function in school. This suggests that if a preadolescent can be helped to gain satisfaction from his schoolroom participation, he may refrain from a predelinquent pattern outside of school. On the basis of this hypothesis, an educationally supportive group-service program was designed.[9]

The Adventure Corps

The Detached Worker and Preadolescent programs used recreational programs and services as a means of involving teen-agers in therapeutic relationships.[10] The combination of services, peer support for socially acceptable attitudes and behavior, and identification with the staff worker were the major means by which the programs were to achieve their goals. The Adventure Corps was designed to serve the same age group as the Preadolescent Program. However, its program activities were viewed as therapeutic ends in themselves. Rather than fit activities to the individual needs of the participants, the program itself made demands on

[9] This program is discussed in detail in the chapter "New Programs for Group Work Agencies" in this volume.

[10] Workers seldom told members directly that the program and services were designed to change their behavior, for fear that members would reject the program service and that all opportunity to help would thus be lost. Some have argued, however, that if the terms of the relationship are not made clear, a great deal of time is wasted and confusion created by attempts to be subtle, while realistic demands on members are likely to be put off.

them, set up standards for conformance, and provided rewards for excellence.

The corps was composed of approximately 350 boys and girls between the ages of nine and thirteen, and approximately fifty more aged thirteen to seventeen. (The older division was added in 1965.) Members of the corps were divided into squads of twenty-five with two divisions of six or seven squads each. Utilizing a paramilitary form, the program content emphasized adventure, discipline, and action.

The program activities were adapted to the interests and general needs of low-income youth, including athletics—judo, wrestling, tumbling, boxing, basketball—camping, marching bands, music—bongo, steel drums—educational programs—narcotics education, tutoring services, trips to museums and theaters—and vocational training programs—trips to industries and trade schools. The corps emphasized squad recognition and awards as well as rewards to individuals. Leadership in the squads was granted to individuals who had demonstrated ability in various corps programs.

It was expected that competition among individuals and squads would result in pressure within the group for conformity to the program's values and goals. A range of programs was made available in order to give each child a chance to succeed in some respect. Parents were encouraged to participate in squad activities through parent advisory groups.

The Adventure Corps Program, like the Detached Worker and Preadolescent programs, was housed in contract agencies, but these agencies were not primarily the large social settlements or community centers of the neighborhood. They were churches, athletic clubs, and small community centers. Recruitment initially was done through the contract agencies, as well as by detached workers.

The contract agencies had minimal experience in sponsoring youth activities. Consequently they were not able to recruit adequate leadership; nor did they see the necessity for following the general guidelines of the corps. After the first year, the director of the Adventure Corps, through various administrative means, assumed more control of the program. By the second year, leaders were supervised and hired by MFY personnel. A training program was run for leaders and considerably more emphasis was placed on the intersquad meetings, the corps group meetings.

The average weekly squad attendance was fourteen. Each squad met once a week for approximately two and a half hours. In addition, each member was required to take part in one other Adventure Corps activity during the week, such as a squad trip, bugle practice session, special drill session, or divisional meeting.

Excerpts from reports of observers indicate the extent to which the program's goals were realized:

> The Adventure Corps' target population was defined as the potentially delinquent boy and girl. Until that concept is more definitively defined, it is difficult to make an accurate assessment of whether delinquent-prone children are being reached by the Adventure Corps. It is my impression that the Adventure Corps is reaching fewer delinquent-prone children than the Preadolescent Program, though most of the children live in an environment that leads to the development of antisocial behavior. . . .

> The uniforms and visibility of the Adventure Corps—marches, parades, divisional meetings—seem to be the basic innovation in the program. If these were taken away, the Adventure Corps would look very much like any other junior division program of a community center or settlement house. The members of the corps enjoy the visibility and recognition they get from these public activities. The corps meetings, where all squads demonstrate their skill in various activties, are generally well attended and add to the satisfaction of being a member of the corps.

> A disquieting factor in the first three years of the program has been the tremendous turnover rate from one program year to the next, averaging around 70 percent. Turnover for the present year in 30 percent. It should be understood that in-out migration in the neighborhood is high.[11]

The Adventure Corps had much success in organizing two parents' groups. These groups were very active in helping with the

[11] The high turnover rate in the early period can also to some extent be attributed to the decentralized administration of the corps during the earlier years as well as to inexperience in its operation.

squads as well as having their own social and educational events. The success of these parents' groups contrasted with the failure of parent groups in the Preadolescent Program and may be related to the fact that in the Adventure Corps, parents were permitted to organize activities for themselves rather than being strictly focused on helping the children.

In the main, leadership of the program was provided by college youths, assisted by local teen-agers. The program was considerably dependent on the quality of this leadership, which seemed to vary from bad to quite good. What the program demonstrated is that there are significant numbers of preadolescents who do not avail themselves of agency facilities. This may occur not because the agency programs are inadequate, but simply because they are not visible and accessible at the times they are needed.

The Adventure Corps also suggested that recreational programs for low-income youth must be glamorous, visible, and, at the same time, related to their everyday experience. While it is difficult to assess the validity of some of the original programmatic ideas for deterring delinquency—drilling, squad competition, paramilitary form, etc.—it is clear that this type of program is attractive. It would seem that lack of visibility of social-settlement and other community agency programs should be rectified.

The Coffee Shop Program

In its first three years of operation Mobilization For Youth opened and subsequently closed two teen-age coffee houses—Club 169 and The Hideout. Over thirty staff members, exclusive of teen-agers, were at one time or another employed in the Coffee House Program, and some three hundred persons between fourteen and twenty-two years of age were served in various ways by the two clubs.

The idea of coffee houses for teen-agers was inspired by a social-cultural movement developed in the 1950's among college students, artists, and intellectuals, who tried to recreate in New York, San Francisco, and other large cities of the United States, the European cafe as a center of intellectual, social, and cultural activities. The success of these transplanted cafes prompted some social workers to adapt the style to a teen-age milieu, as an experiment with delinquency-prone youth. One feature was added—space for dancing—and the famous espresso machine was discarded in favor of a soft-drink vendor. The folk music and modern jazz presented in coffee houses were replaced by records of Latin and rock 'n' roll music; foreign newspapers were replaced by comic books and magazines. Ping-pong and pool tables, hot dogs and soda pop, bus trips and weekly dances were crowded in under the coffee-house banner.

The coffee-shop project, as outlined by the Proposal, was intended to offer members of the neighborhod gangs a neutral turf, a place where they could socialize together on safe ground. The idea was that, if the gang members were offered an opportunity to explore their own interests and culture, and develop their talents in a setting where social workers would be available to help them, the need for conflict and other delinquent behavior would diminish.

In November 1962, six staff members combed the Mobilization area to find suitable facilities. After much searching (landlords were reluctant to lease any facility for use by teen-agers belonging to gangs) Club 169 was set up in a vacant theater on Allen Street.[12] Unfortunately laborious renovation was required. Club 169 finally opened, eight months after the debut of the action program of Mobilization For Youth. Remodeling and equiping a coffee house turned out to be a much greater task than anticipated. While the Allen Street theater had some of the glamour of a night club—street marquee, mirrored mosaic foyer, antique bar, etc.—there were physical drawbacks that made it something of an administrative relief to close it thirteen months later. The rental was high, the building was in a state of dangerous deterioration, a steady flow of funds was required for heating, repair of faulty air conditioning, plumbing, falling plaster, rotten floors, etc. Another problem was that Club 169 was three blocks outside the Mobilization area; many of its members lived beyond the MFY area and

[12] The difficulty of finding adequate facilities in time for the planned opening of activities severely hampered this program. Six months were lost in finding appropriate facilities for the coffee houses. The staff became quite demoralized during this period. In program planning, the problem of finding and maintaining facilities should not be underestimated.

therefore were ineligible for other MFY services, until a plan was worked out to accept some of them in these other programs on a percentage basis.

Shortly after renting the Allen Street location, the first and second stories of a four-story loft building, formerly used as a laundry, were leased for the second coffee house, named The Hideout. The renovation, performed by members of the Urban Youth Corps, included pouring a new concrete floor, laying tiles, installing new plumbing and electricity, a heating system, partitions, new walls and ceilings, constructing closets and cabinets, and reframing windows. Four gangs were invited to The Hideout—the Sportsmen, the Eastmen Dragons, the Untouchables, and the Comanches.[13]

Each group was approached through its peer leaders, with the assistance of Youth Board workers. Coffee-house workers spent the first months on the streets getting to know the boys and assessing their opinions on belonging to a coffee house which would involve them in direct contact with rival gangs. All of them expressed reluctance. Privately, they told workers about past gang fights and why one group had fought another. Some of them held grudges against individual members of certain groups and could not fully accept the group for that reason.

The purpose of forming a council was discussed with the leaders of each gang at separate meetings; then followed several meetings of the council. Subsequently, members of all four groups met at an MFY storefront on 4th Street for the first time. There were no incidents. The opening of The Hideout was also uneventful; cultural activities had already been taking place on the second floor while the downstairs recreation area was under construction.

The council, or board of managers, was able to function for a short period. However, it labored under unanticipated handicaps. Several members were arrested and sent to jail; two others, drug users, were consistently absent; there was intergroup bickering at meetings as one group or another was accused of attempting to usurp leadership. Above all, there was a natural tendency for groups to isolate themselves within the shop. The idea that the gang leaders would form a peer prestige group did not succeed.

[13] The history of Club 169 closely paralleled that of The Hideout.

Although they tolerated each other within the setting, their communication did not extend beyond The Hideout walls. The cultural program appealed to small subgroups but did not succeed in improving intergroup relations. There was a good deal of drinking on dance nights, and a number of boys, including the leaders, arrived at the club high on alcohol or narcotics. It became clear that the council was unable to function as a positive standard-bearing group since the prestige of most of its members had been achieved and was maintained primarily through antisocial activities.

On the question of drinking, drugs, and fighting, the board of managers drew up a set of rules which was distributed among the membership and posted on bulletin boards. Drinking and drugs remained a problem in both coffee houses, contrary to the Proposal's optimistic prediction:

> Youth aged eighteen or older who are legally permitted to drink, have had special difficulty accepting the ban on alcohol in most community centers. The Coffee Shop format mitigates this problem since it is well known that no coffee shop in the city is allowed to serve or permit the drinking of alcohol.[14]

The drinking and drug problem, on the contrary, reached such proportions in Club 169 that it had to be closed down for a time.

Stronger measures were enforced during the first year of The Hideout; members who exhibited overt symptoms of drug usage were suspended from the program. This did not enhance relationships between staff members and other members. It must be kept in mind that the shops were created for the most disturbed and disorganized of the adolescent population, almost all of whom had experience with marijuana, illegal drinking, pep pills, cocaine, or heroin.[15] It was naïve to believe that a social-cultural program would eradicate this pattern.

[14] *A Proposal for the Prevention and Control of Delinquency by Expanding Opportunities* (New York, Mobilization For Youth, 1961), p. 396.

[15] Staff was of course concerned lest those whom the program was designed to serve would be kept out. The need to maintain some balance between too much control and too much disorder was a recurring and ultimately insoluble problem. One of the earliest manifestations of this problem was the police practice of entering the coffee house looking for suspected offenders.

An incident between a fringe member of the Sportsmen and a Commanche was the sole disturbance among the member groups; yet it almost precipitated the renewal of gang warfare. Immediate action by Hideout staff and Youth Board workers resulted in a settlement. Luring this crisis, The Hideout was closed for two weeks.

Many staff members expressed the feeling that The Hideout was a dynamite keg, especially on the frequent occasions when nonmembers wished to gain entrance and were denied. The fact that The Hideout membership consisted of potentially destructive youngsters who often attracted other delinquency-prone individuals and groups made control of the premises an arduous task. Rarely an evening passed without a scene at the door involving a staff member, a member, and a nonmember. Such occasions did not elevate the morale of the staff, and worse yet, the more peace-loving members began to avoid the premises. By spring, the attendance consisted primarily of drug users.

The provision of individual counseling services proved to be a mammoth task. Many members of The Hideout needed help, and a worker often spent an entire evening with a single individual. The Proposal anticipated that the coffee shops would eventually become referral centers to resources needed by adolescents: "In the natural setting of the youth, professional staff, acting as 'informal bartenders,' can offer on-the-spot guidance and referral to youngsters in need of educational, vocational, or psychiatric assistance." [16]

This function was carried out fully in The Hideout program. Workers held nightly conferences on obtaining employment, holding a job, remaining in school, seeking individual services, medical care, improving family relations, etc. The worker's day was spent in court, in jail, in school, in pursuit of job counselors, caseworkers, lawyers, probation officers, truant officers, Youth Board workers, and teachers, along with the regular obligations to attend staff meetings and conferences.

One important finding in the coffee-house program was that almost every client asking for help with one problem had many

[16] *A Proposal for the Prevention and Control of Delinquency by Expanding Opportunities* (New York, Mobilization For Youth, 1961), p. 397.

others requiring immediate attention. A teen-ager requesting help in finding a job might also have an upcoming trial for petty theft, a history of drug use, a venereal disease, family problems, etc.[17]

Gang wars made no history during the 1963–64 season on the Lower East Side. There was no longer a need for coffee shops for gangs, and the policy was revised for the following season to permit open membership. A general announcement was sent to all members registered in 1963–64 that the coffee houses were now open on an individual-participation basis. Some 140 boys and fifty girls registered for The Hideout. Of these 190 registrants, one hundred attended fewer than five times from November to May. Approximately fifty of the remaining ninety showed a regular attendance record. The staff consisted of two full-time group workers, three part-time specialists—photography, leather craft, and music or drama—a part-time receptionist, and three teen-age employees—a part-time counterman, record-room aide, and checkroom attendant. With this smaller and less delinquency-prone membership, staff achieved a division of labor. Programmatic improvements were notable. The assistant director was assigned to a volunteer council which, in effect, represented a fairly homogeneous membership. Most of the participants were Negroes, many of them from East River housing projects. Of the four groups in the original program, the Sportsmen were the only ones to continue on a regular basis. Most of them were involved with marijuana and other narcotics, and those who frequented the shop in a state of intoxication were suspended. Several held grudges against the staff for this action and were a perpetual nuisance throughout the year, attempting to gain entrance to The Hideout, threatening staff members, and encouraging drug usage among younger members. At all times there were attempts on the part of older members to peddle drugs in the shop, and since this was

[17] A problem endemic to most MFY programs was the overwhelming difficulty of providing clients with the individual services they needed. (See the chapter "From Reform School to Society" in this volume for an analysis of this problem.) Certainly one of the reasons for MFY's stance in regard to the need for reform of institutions which serve the poor lies in the fact that to begin to meet all the needs of a single multiproblem family would require the full-time services of a worker. Even if needs could be met on an individual basis, if the situations which caused most of the needs remained unaltered, the cycle of need would start again.

done in clandestine ways, staff members were unable to fix blame on any particular person. All those who were under suspicion were eventually arrested on drug, mugging, or larceny charges, and temporarily put out of circulation.

The coffee-shop program was closed in the spring of 1965. The individuals who attented it its last year were not those whom it was set up to serve. In the fall of 1965, a cultural arts program and an Adolescent Service Center were set up to fill the gap in the agency's program.[18]

There are several conclusions which may be derived from the coffee-shop experience. It is likely that drug addiction is a form of deviance which is so debilitating that addicts cannot be successfully integrated in programs, recreational or other. The coffee shops simply could not contain the drug addicts. Furthermore, the assumption that the Greenwich Village coffee shop is a model for delinquent youth is tenuous. The expectation that youth would not want to drink in the coffee shops simply because alcohol is not served in the Greenwich Village coffee shops was not borne out.

The power of the peer managerial group was never developed. If the renovation of the coffee shops had been done by the member groups themselves rather than by the Urban Youth Corps, new forms of leadership might have emerged, based on the contributions made to the overall coffee-shop program. This might have displaced the existing gang leadership or at least transformed the basis of leadership into one that was conformist. Instead, the first problem-solving activities to confront the groups centered around power and control over the coffee shops. In this context, competition between established groups naturally emerged.[19] It seemed so important to get deviant groups inside the coffee shop that they were brought in at the price of nonconformity.

[18] These programs are described in the chapters on "Training Youth in the Arts" and "Adolescent Service Centers" both in this volume.

[19] Probably a more effective approach would have been for the staff initially to act as the managers and rule-setters, with teen-agers as advisers; and then gradually turn over the management to the teen-agers. During this period of transition, "town hall" meetings of all members might have been a better tactic for letting new leadership emerge than immediately setting up a council.

Finally, the failure of the Coffee Shop Program is not an indication that the settlements should not have "lounge" type programs. What it does show is that expectations of what can be achieved in these programs is rather limited in terms of loosening peer-group control over members, transforming subcultural values, and introducing new programmatic activities.

Conclusions

The boys sat around the table waiting to be interviewed. They were members of a Detached Group—an ex-gang—now being served by one of the settlement houses. The interviewer explained that she was from Mobilization For Youth and wanted to talk to them about what had happened since they had been given a social worker and met in the settlement. They were asked to talk about their gang days and compare them to how they spent their time now. The members looked around at each other, shifted in their chairs, and eventually began to talk. They said that they liked their social worker—he was a "good guy"; he let them use the gym for basketball practice and for games. They said that they came to the the settlement once or twice a week to use the gym or to plan a trip or "something." They said they didn't like sitting around and talking—"it was boring." In response to questions about the "old days," they said, yes, they were exciting, but too risky. Risk was defined as "too much chance of going to jail" and "you could get killed out there." When asked what happened to stop them from bopping, they said, "Everyone else stopped." When asked what they would recommend to help keep kids out of trouble, they said, "Keep the kids off the street."

Gang warfare had largely subsided on the Lower East Side before Mobilization actually began operating. Some possible reasons were: (1) the increase of narcotics use, a more passive mode of rebelling against society; (2) pressure mounted by the police, resulting in many arrests and sentencing of gang members; and (3) the community response to the problem, as the Youth Board and other social agencies offered a way out, an alternative behavior pattern. The gangs were given social workers and places to meet. Someone was paying attention to them. Yet delinquency did not subside.

A number of conclusions about the effect of group work and recreation on delinquents can be drawn from the experience in the four programs described. The attempt to use group programs as socializing mechanisms generally proved unsuccessful. The value of the purposeful use of group activities and group structure (i.e. group work) as a prevention or a cure for delinquency is open to question. While such methods and processes can harness peer support and can make possible a relationship of trust between members and group workers, most of the problems of the delinquent and delinquency-prone are not amenable to solutions solely within the confines of a group. MFY's experience shows that the single most effective and socially useful way of helping a delinquent youth was to provide him with immediate and concrete assistance with his personal problems.[20]

It seems apparent that the chief contribution of recreational agencies and facilities, while attempting to provide healthy social and emotional experiences, is to "keep the kids off the street." This should not be overlooked or denigrated as a contribution to the prevention of delinquency. The gang members themselves repeatedly referred to the value of having a place to go where they would not get into trouble.

The staff workers seem to have functioned quite adequately as social brokers. There is clearly a need for an understanding and concerned adult to be available to delinquency-prone youth. MFY's work-training program and legal department were valuable resources for the detached workers. Good relationships between staff of social agencies and delinquents need to be buttressed by real job, educational, and social opportunities.

The Coffee Shop and Detached Worker programs were viewed as ports of entry into Mobilization. This was their only source of integration with the other MFY programs. It may be that the programs would have been more effective had they been regarded not as ports of entry, but as rewards for successful experience in other parts of the program. For example, membership in the coffee

[20] Manipulating group processes can be useful in marshaling peer-group support for members seeking and using the help offered.

shops might have been restricted to those gainfully employed in the world of work.

MFY programs were not sequentially related, one to the other, as part of an ordered and total resocialization process—e.g., leading from work training to permanent employment to the coffee shop, to the managerial group of a coffee shop or a young-adult action group. MFY opted for a dispersed, fragmented program approach to reach as many adolescents as possible rather than to involve fewer in depth, in some form of total resocialization process.

An agency with MFY's resources might consider a saturation socialization experience directed through its programs at the full range of statuses and activities in which adolescents participate—work, education, family, peer group. To achieve this goal, an agency would have to restrict its rules of eligibility and clearly delimit its target groups.

The Detached Worker, Preadolescent and Coffee Shop programs essentially used their recreation component as enticement for the establishment of a relationship between worker and member. They did not really consider the part recreation and play assume in a delinquent's life, other than as substitutes for antisocial activities. Only the Adventure Corps attempted to address itself to the central issue of "play in life." Although it may be argued that play and recreation should be regarded as rewards for other, more meaningful or socially useful activities, on the other hand, the increasing technological and automated development of society puts into question the whole work orientation of society. Our present delinquents may represent the avant garde of groups for whom neither work nor play, as currently conceived, can serve as a point of reference with society.

9

Programs for the Adolescent Addict

Beverly Luther

At a time when a youth is expected to be anticipating completing secondary education, thinking and planning about a vocational future, and trying out in fantasy various adult roles, the street addict has dropped out of high school and has become overwhelmingly dependent on drugs. Becoming an addict results in a complete reorientation of roles, in that hustling for drugs utilizes all the youth's resources. As a consequence, he has little energy or time available for the development of essential skills in the working world or in other forms of living. The adolescent narcotics addict, in addition to being dependent on drugs, is involved in a subculture which is totally involved in activities to obtain drugs, mostly through illegal activities. These activities are partially supported by the community in which he is living, in that addicts obtain income by selling stolen consumer goods to impoverished housewives.[1]

Drug addiction on the Lower East Side was not a serious problem until the late 1950's, when gangs of Italian and Irish youths turned from fighting off the inroads of Negro and Puerto Rican newcomers to using and pushing heroin. By 1961 the block on Henry Street between Montgomery and Clinton streets was known as Junkies' Paradise. Personnel of the Lower East Side Neighborhoods Association Narcotics Information Center, with offices on that block, estimated that more than fifty addicts regularly hung around the block, and that about fifteen of these people were

[1] Lower East Side Narcotics Information Center, "Five Year Evaluation" (mimeographed, New York, 1967), p. 85.

136

pushers. Some gangs known to the settlement houses during the intensive gang-fighting phase were already addicted to heroin.

Although the increasing use of narcotics on the Lower East Side was known at the time the Proposal was written, no program was designed to deal specifically with the drug problem.[2] One reason was that the Proposal applied the same theoretical base to all delinquents. If delinquent youths were provided with legitimate opportunities for stable social roles, educational advancement, and occupational choice, it was thought that their deviant behavior, whether in the form of assault, theft, or addiction, would diminish. Nevertheless, for the past five years, Mobilization has dealt with the problems of narcotics addiction in various ways. This paper will describe programs especially designed for the addict as well as programs aimed at the general delinquent population which have some relation to the prevention and cure of addiction.

The Work Programs

When Mobilization's programs of vocational training, on-the-job training, and direct-placement services started, there was a small percentage of addicts among the applicants. In 1963, forty-five known addicts were participating in this program. As work crews formed and training intensified, addict trainees became a real problem. Absenteeism, lateness, "nodding" on the job, trembling hands, confused thinking, and, in some instances, drug pushing, plus the manipulative, dependent, and demanding characteristics of the addict, led the staff to reevaluate how best to serve the addict in a work-training program.

At first work-trainee addicts were referred to the Lower East Side Narcotics Information Center for intensive help while continuing to participate in the training program. The plan was to structure and coordinate the demands made on the addict to ensure a more consistent approach to his problem and to prevent him from setting worker against worker. Few of the training staff had had previous experience working with addicts. Some were

[2] The Proposal noted that a contract would be given to the Lower East Side Narcotics Information Center to develop programs for the addict.

too permissive or inconsistent because of their lack of experience and tended to be deceived by the addicts.

The work-program staff spent many hours attempting to co-ordinate an approach to helping the addict, as well as offering the special services which individuals needed—helping the addict to enter detoxification, procuring legal services, and referring the addict and his family for appropriate social-work help.

The crew chiefs continued to report the disruptive influence of addicts on their work-training groups. The vocational counselors were spending a disproportionate amount of time on addicts in their caseload. In 1963, the work-training program decided to ser-vice only addicts who had been detoxified for six months. Addicts were, in effect, no longer to be served in the work program.

The Coffee Shops

The coffee shops, established in early 1963, were Mobilization's second encounter with the addict population. Here again, MFY eventually closed its doors to addicts. In the beginning the two coffee shops restricted membership to members of known gangs, including addicted members. The actual number of addicts par-ticipating in the program was not known; staff often said that it was difficult for them to tell whether an individual was high on dope or on alcohol.

Both drinking and dope were discussed with the coffee-house councils (peer leadership groups), which agreed to suspend tem-porarily persons who were obviously high and not behaving themselves. Nevertheless, the staff began to have severe control problems. Members of the leadership group would arrive high and begin to act up. Marijuana smoking in the bathrooms was common, and soon some of the addicts began to use the premises of the coffee houses for pushing. The staff was gravely concerned lest nonusers become introduced to dope at the coffee houses. One gang refused to come to the coffee house because they said that it was run by a bunch of junkies.

As was true of the work-program staff, the staff of the coffee houses had moved quickly to offer help to the addict, and found the task endless. Finally, at a meeting of the membership of one coffee house, the staff told the youths that addicts would henceforth be excluded from the program but that Mobilization was working on a plan to help the addicts. The plan became the Group Abstinence Program, known as GAP.

Community Development

Among Mobilization's many direct experiences with addicts in other programs, one evolved out of a community-organization storefront located on 4th Street. Although they were not specifically geared to service addicts, staff tried to help the drug users and addicts who came into the store. They referred addicts to the Narcotics Information Center, took them to appointments at various hospitals, obtained legal help when needed, went to court with them, and on occasion rushed them to hospitals.

In the fall of 1963, an ex-addict who lived on the street came to the community organizers with a plan to establish a Cold Turkey Shelter for addicts. He wanted the shelter located right on 4th Street—a street with a heavy addict population. He was able to interest a few other residents but found it almost impossible to recruit people to sit with an addict during the withdrawal process. A major upheaval resulted when he obtained a tentative commitment from a home owner next door to a public school for the use of his basement. A series of emergency meetings was held by the principal of the school and officers of the PTA. The community organizer was visited by several police officers, including the captain of the precinct, to find out what the shelter was all about. The offer of the basement was quickly withdrawn as pressure mounted on the home owner.

The community organizer, in his report on the Cold Turkey Shelter, ironically commented: "It is interesting that these institutions' response to a widespread problem, which everyone claims is so terrible, is to do nothing about it. The principal of the school sat in her office stating that the establishment of this clinic would attract addicts to 4th Street. The very doorstep of her school is being used by addicts to sit on; her schoolyard had been, was, and continues to be a place where addicts gather in great numbers. . . ." The shelter was abandoned, but the storefront continued for a time to be used as a meeting place by a small group of ex-addicts. Ultimately they set up their own storefront, ostensibly to help other addicts, but it soon evolved into a social club.

The Group Abstinence Program (GAP)

The Group Abstinence Program was created in part because of Mobilization's growing realization of the scope of the drug problem on the Lower East Side, in part because the operation of programs designed to help the youth of the community was obviously being impaired by the inclusion of addicts. Mobilization's executive staff had investigated Synanon, a California-based organization, which had established the fact that, with drugs as with alcohol, a group could often abstain collectively even though no member of it was able to abstain on his own. This idea of group abstinence was chosen as GAP's principal tool.

The program was based on the notion of having a group of young male addicts, under the around-the-clock direction of a staff of social workers, make a common resolution to abstain completely from all drug use, with the understanding that any member who broke the resolution at any subsequent stage of the program would be summarily dropped. Next they would enter a hospital to be detoxified; then go to a camp for a period of six weeks to get back on their feet, then return to New York, where the members would live and receive job training together. The group which was to be the nucleus of the experiment had been a conflict gang and then later had all become addicted. The boys had been hanging around together for over five years and called themselves the Continentals. Seven Continentals and five other recruits entered the hospital for detoxification on June 29, 1964. Their story, as reported by Robert Rice in *The New Yorker* of March 27, 1965, is as follows: [1]

> On the second day in the hospital, three signed themselves out. A few days later, a fourth left. A week and a half after that, the fifth left. All seven Continentals stuck it out for the full three weeks. The hospital had predicted, on the basis of its experience and records, that, of the twelve boys who started, one quarter

[1] Reprinted by permission; © 1965 *The New Yorker Magazine, Inc.*

would finish, so at the end of its first stage the project was well ahead of the game. . . .

I think it is accurate to summarize the six weeks that the boys spent at camp as a series of preliminary tests of whether there was any chance that a group that had come together for strictly anti-social purposes could reverse its character. The least demanding of the tests was remaining physically independent of heroin. . . . Another test that the boys did quite well at was work. There was only one persistent goof-off when it came to bedmaking, floor-sweeping, table-setting, dishwashing, lawn-moving, and other routine duties, and for this his fellows persistently punished him by giving him extra details.

About halfway through camp, the director of the project from Mobilization arranged with the New York City Department of Water Supply, Gas and Electricity for the boys to work mornings at $1.25 an hour, clearing brush around a city reservoir near the camp. It was an inspiration because, after a first flurry with the rowboats and canoes and the swimming pool and the gym, the boys had relapsed into spending their free time listening to the juke-box in the dining hall (they had put it in working order on their second day) or the hi-fi in the recreation hall (they had set this up on their third day) or the radios in their cabins (they had brought these along), and playing cards interminably. One reason for this was that the two staff members, however proficient they may have been in other skills, proved to have few gifts as recreation directors. Everyone except Harry (names falsified), who has never liked to exert himself, turned to at the reservoir with such enthusiasm that the foreman, who had been doubtful at first about his new hands, had to beg them to take it easy, so they wouldn't make the regular crews look bad. . . .

Toward each other the boys behaved, as they always had, quite honorably. As a group, however, they relapsed quite often into scheming, hustling and stealing. One day, they decided that their sleeping cabin was too austerely furnished, so they broke into some locked cabins and "found" various chests of drawers and carpets that they fancied. . . . Drinking also continued to break out. . . .

The two staff members were put to a stiff test themselves—working harmoniously together for nine weeks in the cramped environment of a hospital ward and a mountain camp with only ex-junkies and each other for company. They didn't pass it. . . . They tried to keep their differences to themselves, but the boys, of course, sensed them at once and took advantage of them, constantly appealing to one social worker over the head of the other. The issue finally had to be resolved by returning one to New York. . . .

The departure of this staff member occurred two weeks before the end of camp, when all the currents and cross currents I have mentioned, and probably a lot I didn't detect, combined [to produce mounting tension] boredom of camp life, the wrangles over money, the difficulties between the two staff members, the boys' increasing awareness that giving up heroin was going to involve not only "feeling good" but accepting discipline and facing everyday problems they had never dared face before, like work and education and family life, and even sex—for the sex life of a junkie is usually as dim as the rest of his life. It is my belief, moreover, that they had an even more unsettling problem than any of these to deal with. As a group of addicts, their personalities had been blurred and their many differences in intelligence and temperament had not been evident. But once they had been sober for a couple of months they scarcely knew each other any more. In short, the group was breaking up. . . .

On the morning of the last day of camp. . . . the boys were clearly pleased to be leaving the sticks, although they weren't nearly as exuberant as they had been on certain less noteworthy occasions when I had been with them. They seemed to have been sobered by their camp experience, which, of course, was precisely its object. They seemed uneasily aware, besides, that the purpose of the city experience they were embarking upon was to sober them more. . . . When we crossed Fourteenth Street, the boys came to life and began eagerly pointing out spots of interest, which were mostly scenes of gang fights they had been in. . . .

Upon their arrival at temporary quarters (Mobilization had not secured a permanent group living house), all the boys rushed upstairs to shower, shave, and change into clean clothes; they had permission to visit home that night, with orders to be back by one in the morning. A few minutes later, they streamed merrily out into Henry Street, scrubbed and brushed and combed until they glistened, on the way to give their parents their first look in years at what their sons were like sober. Then and there, at ten minutes to eight on the evening of Tuesday, September 1, 1964, on the sidewalk in front of 46 Henry Street, the Continentals were closer than they had ever been to having it made, and closer than they have ever been since. . . .

By January the project was dead. One by one the boys had drifted back to heroin. The staff of Mobilization is still debating the Group Abstinence Program two years after it officially failed. There seems to be general agreement that the idea was good but that it was poorly implemented. The consensus is that it was a mistake to bring in non-Continentals—they did not belong to the group, and, after all, it was the concept of group cohesiveness that was to be tested as the method of abstaining from drugs. Another mistake was the failure to assess the specific educational and vocational training needs of each boy and to plan with the boy to meet these needs. An obvious mistake was the lack of preparation for the return of the boys from camp. Mobilization had great difficulty acquiring a suitable residence for the boys when they came back to the city. Nevertheless, preparation for the whole project should have included obtaining the hospital facilities, the camp, and the halfway house prior to launching the project.

From the point of view of social-work techniques, a crucial error was the failure of the staff and project to stand firmly on the contract made with the boys—expulsion for those who went back on drugs. The first exception to the rule set the tone for the group: "If they don't mean what they say, we can continue scheming, hustling and lying." A further error was the staff's failure to predict and plan for changes in group structure once detoxification had been accomplished.

There were also problems in coordinating the efforts of various divisions of Mobilization. At one time or another the divisions of Group Services, Community Development, and Employment Opportunities plus the top executives of MFY were all involved in this program. The project director constantly argued the need for his own vocational counselors, teachers, etc., so that the total operation would have one administrative locale.[3]

[3] In fairness to the administration, the problems involved in this program were imense and manifold. For instance, after a camp site was rented in New Jersey, it was found that addicts could not be transported to it without a cumbersome registration procedure with the local police, and a new camp site had to be found.

It was initially hypothesized that the success of GAP would depend on peer support and the cohesiveness of the group. According to Rice's account, the old gang structure was threatened once the group was detoxified and taken out of their familiar surroundings—they were confronted by strangers. This was equivalent to a double shock; getting to know themselves without drugs was difficult enough, but now their long-time, once predictable friends were new people too.

The Lower East Side Narcotics Information Center

From 1962 to 1967, Mobilization helped to fund the Lower East Side Narcotics Information Center, which had been started by LENA (Lower East Side Neighborhoods Association) in the late 1950's. The contract was to fund a multidisciplinary neighborhood treatment center for narcotics addicts, especially those between the ages of fourteen and twenty-one. The original goal was to see whether such an approach could improve the lives of the addicts and bring some to a state where they could abstain from narcotics.

The multidisciplinary approach means the use of social workers, psychologists, psychiatrists, vocational counselors, volunteers, etc., all working together as a team, in behalf of the client. The center utilized a combination of techniques: concrete help with the addict's external reality problems; social planning in order to improve his functioning toward some stated goal; and insight therapy, developing a sustained relationship with the addict in order to help him with long-term planning.

> The addict is an individual who, while under the influence of drugs, is relatively free from anxiety and as a result is not approachable in terms of psychotherapeutic treatment. . . . He is more aware of the numerous social, personal and economic problems with which he cannot deal and which are very real. . . . Addicts can best be reached and helped, at least at the outset, on the level of concrete and tangible services . . . these services [are] the only appropriate ones to help ease pressures on patient and family, build a case-

work relationship and ultimately involve the addict more meaning-fully.[4]

Contact with a typical client would start in the waiting room of the center. The intake worker saw the addict first and filled out a long information form, including the client's definition of his prob-lem. If he wished the center's help in getting to a hospital for de-toxification, as was usually the case, an appointment was made at the hospital for him. Most addicts stayed at the hospital less than the four weeks required for total detoxification.

At the time of discharge, the hospital would phone the center and make an appointment for the addict. The majority of addicts did not keep this posthospital appointment but would show up at the center four to six months later with a new presenting problem —usually trouble with probation or parole, the courts or welfare. If he did not wish detoxification, the addict was assigned a worker to help him with his presenting problem. Usually when the im-mediate problem was solved (unless the client was mandated to treatment by probation or parole), the client would disappear once more. He would reappear at the next crisis and go through the same procedure—disappearing and returning many times. Dur-ing one of these crisis contacts, some clients would begin to talk about their more personal goals and difficulties, at which time social planning would begin. The center staff would intervene di-rectly with the public authorities—welfare, parole, etc.—to take unrealistic pressures off the client. Most of the clients at this time would not be abstaining from drugs. As a relationship developed between the worker and the addict, and as the addict developed some capacity for self-assertion, other services were supplied, such as tutoring, vocational counseling, evening recreation, and encouragement to use community facilities. When the addict reached this stage, the counseling became more like therapy.

The addict was referred for employment and job training at his request. The center discovered in its first years of operation that the addict was not usually ready for these steps; at present, staff spend a good deal of time exploring with him his readiness for

[4] Lower East Side Narcotics Information Center, *op. cit.*, p. 37, 39.

such activities. When both addict and staff feel that the addict is ready, jobs and job training are provided, as well as more concrete services—help with housing, etc. If the addict is still living at home during this time, the center staff aggressively seeks to improve the family atmosphere or encourages the addict to leave home if the family is uncooperative. Some addicts continue in counseling for a number of months, others drop out but return again for help with another external crisis or "for more talk." Despite all this activity, the results in terms of rehabilitated addicts have been unimpressive.

A five-year evaluation of the center's work included the following appraisal:

> Older addicts (over 25) would appear to be more responsive to long range planning. . . . Our experience suggests that adolescent drug users are most unlikely to desire to relinquish drugs and to be able to plan sufficiently ahead. . . .[5]

Caseload Composition 1962–1967

SEX

Males	870
Females	142

ETHNICITY

Puerto Rican	470
Negro	191
White (other)	271
Chinese	39
Unknown	41

MARITAL STATUS

Married	336
Single	539
Unknown	137

[5] The evaluation notes that there is a large group of former addicts who appear to "mature out" of addiction—that is, they experience a realization that their pattern of living is taking them nowhere and for no apparent external reason discontinue the use of drugs. *Ibid.*, p. 87.

AGE

15–19	139
20–24	335
25–29	211
Over 30	285
Unknown	42

Although the center was intended to serve the adolescent addict, most of the clients who sought out its services were at least twenty years old. The adolescent addict is much less likely to seek help for his addiction, in part because he regards it as only temporary— "I have lots of time to play around"—and believes that he can quit whenever he wants to. The adult, on the other hand, is likely to find that his addiction seriously hampers his ability to attain such goals as stable employment, supporting a family, etc. When he realizes that these goals are unreachable because of his addiction, the adult seeks help.

In 1964, in response to the limited results achieved with adolescent addicts, a storefront was opened by the center on East 5th Street [6] to provide recreation and group services for preadolescent glue sniffers, and a variety of concrete services for adolescents who used heroin sporadically. Neighborhood adults were recruited to assist in the work of the storefront and to refer potential addicts to it.

The program revealed that there was considerable variation among adolescents in the frequency and type of drug use as well as in reaction to such use. The neighborhood atmosphere clearly affected adolescent perception of drugs. A three-year evaluation of this program contained the following suggestions:

It is our observation that most of the substance users with whom we have regular contact have made a marginal adaptation to their social environment. . . . Only three members can be considered addicted to heroin. Of these three, two work regularly. The others— no matter which substance they use, heroin, glue, marijuana, liquor

[6] The center carried on a number of other projects and activities, from research on methadone usage to training graduate students in a variety of disciplines. See *ibid.*

—appear to have a need to be "high" as a result of a cultural expectation. For young people of this age and in these neighborhoods being "high" is the socially "hip" thing to do, just as gang membership was ten years ago.

Although it is difficult if not impossible to prove, we believe that working on the block over the past two and a half years has had some influence on enabling the target-group members to maintain at least a marginal adaptation. It is our hope that even by just "holding the line" we can help provide a moratorium for our adolescent members until the maturation processes enable them to outgrow the need for participation in the "hip" way of life on the streets.

An even more difficult thing to measure is the possible influence the accessibility and visibility of the block-approach program has had in the community regarding attitudes toward narcotic addiction and its prevention. We believe that the example of an agency and its workers committed to the cause of narcotics-use prevention and cure had a positive effect on the attitudes of the people in the community.[7]

Conclusion

A recent study by Mobilization of various treatment approaches to addiction showed that the major efforts are being conducted within the state correctional systems. Additional efforts are being financed by voluntary agencies, church groups, and psychiatric clinics, many of which have received funding grants from the National Institute of Mental Health or from the Department of Health, Education, and Welfare. In correctional programs the main emphasis is on group therapy for the inmates and job training, plus various after-release services. The smaller agencies are experimenting with many approaches, including the intensive use of psychotherapy, family therapy, vocational counseling, and group therapy. Several hospitals throughout the country have programs substituting the less habit-forming and less expensive narcotic methadone for heroin.

[7] Lower East Side Narcotics Information Center, "Block-Approach Progress Report" (mimeographed, New York, 1965).

The best-known new approach for the treatment of addiction is the method used at Synanon. New York has an equivalent to Synanon in Day Top Lodge. The addict's chances of relinquishing the habit permanently, however, still remain bleak. The statistics on recidivism are overwhelming.

Despite the failure of Mobilization's various attempts to serve addicts, there are several conclusions that can be drawn from the MFY experience which may assist future addiction programs.

When an individual is an addict, not just a user or an experimenter, his need is not merely for job training or a place to socialize. Training or rehabilitation can begin only after detoxification. Addicts should not be admitted to programs designed for non-addicts until they are detoxified; once clean, they should be expelled if they go back on drugs. Firm authority is required. Their admittance to any program should be carefully considered. Prior to their admittance, realistic demands of behavior should be placed on addicts, so that they prove to staff and more important, to themselves, that they can make it.

The experiences in the work-training and coffee-shop programs indicate the need for a specifically designed, well-planned program for addicts which requires first detoxification and second rehabilitation. Rehabilitation for the addict must begin with the belief that cure is possible. One way of instilling this belief is by confronting him with former addicts who have successfully kicked the habit. Motivation is the key to the treatment of any emotional illness. If motivation is lacking, all the services and therapies known will continue to fail.

Some form of group support seems necessary to keep the addict from backsliding. The Group Abstinence Program suggests that a halfway house is an important factor in the rehabilitation of the adolescent addict. The program really fell apart when such a facility could not be established.

Mobilization's experience also suggests that experimentation with drugs begins very early in the life of the Lower East Side slum child. Very little has been done in the area of prevention. One suggestion is to saturate the public schools, beginning at the third-grade levels, with audio-visual material designed to educate children concerning the danger of narcotics addiction. The problem is massive; only massive preventive and treatment methods can have any perceptible effect.

10

Negro Youth and Social Action

Beverly Luther

The experience in some southern cities of a decrease in delinquent acts attendant on an increase in civil-rights activities [1] was the theoretical rationale for MFY's decision in November 1963 to begin organizing a social-action group of low-income Puerto Rican and Negro teen-agers. The Proposal had also suggested the development of a young-adult social-action group in an attempt to shift the frustration and anger of low-income minority-group adolescents into constructive activity directed to problems faced by the entire community. [2] It was hoped that a youth-action group by its example would help to overcome the social apathy of both youths and adults in the community. This paper will describe the history of a group organized for these purposes, called the Young Adult Action Group (YAAG).

The Program Phase

The ten youngsters who comprised the original core group were recruited by staff members who had contact with delinquent and delinquency-prone youth. The recruiters found that the general

[1] This correlation was reported in Fredric Soloman et al., "Civil Rights Activity and Reduction in Crime Among Negroes," *Archives of General Psychiatry*, Vol. 12. (March 1965). The conclusions of this study have been questioned on the ground that the situation reflects the fact that the police were busy with civil rights and had less time for criminal work.

[2] *A Proposal for the Prevention and Control of Delinquency by Expanding Opportunities*, (New York, Mobilization for Youth, 1961), p. 171.

concept of the group had to be explained carefully, since most of the potential members had no frame of reference for social action. The core group, not all of whom had known each other, brought their friends, who brought their friends, and thus the group grew quickly. Officers were elected, committees formed, and a program planned. Attendance at meetings varied from around twenty-five to thirty. The age of the members varied from enighteen to twenty-two. During the first year Young Adult Action Group sponsored a food drive for Mississippi, put out a newspaper sporadically, participated in school-integration protests, and demonstrated for passage of civil-rights and youth-employment legislation, locally and in Washington, D.C. The staff during this year consisted of three full-time workers—two male white, one female white—and one part-time male Negro. The group's ethnic composition started out as mixed, with both Negro and Puerto Rican members. As the year continued, the group became increasingly Negro, reflecting the Negro program emphasis.

By late fall of 1964 attendance had dropped off severely. Tensions had begun to develop between the more delinquency-prone youths and the more conventional types. More and more staff had to control disruptions at meetings. By September 1965 the group had essentially disintegrated and was completely dependent on staff for its survival. The Negro staff member described the failure of the group as follows:

There was in fact no program that was successful. A number of events were—the trips to Washington, a dance, an evening-long meeting with kids from Mississippi up North under the sponsorship of SNCC. But these were all events, they were all tactics. They were not things that had any organic relationship to each other. There was no concrete programmatic development. Program had to be manufactured, and you cannot continually manufacture program. As a result, a number of unfortunate things began to occur.

Staff began to lose control to the exact degree that we did not deal with the essence of who the youths were; which is the same as saying refusal to recognize the essence of their humanity.

We were also losing control in a very pragmatic sense. These teenagers . . . were very quick to pick up things, and thus testing began. A vacuum developed into which staff threw more and more middle-class white ideas in order to stem the tide, such as food for Mississippi. These kids were not interested in sending food to Mississippi, they were interested in going to Mississippi. . . .

This analysis of the group's problems was the one that was ultimately accepted, though others were offered.[3] Many noted that the fate of the Young Adult Action Group seemed to be directly related to the problems of the civil-rights movement. The general letdown felt by ciivl-rights organizations in the North following the passage of the Civil Rights Act was experienced in the group. Disillusionment with the slow pace of change had an effect on the organization.

Another hypothesis was that the projects in the past were in the main symbolic, that they did not deal with the real problems youths were facing on the Lower East Side. Just before the food drive for Mississippi, the group had a discussion which could be summed up as "I don't want to just shake the President's hand." The staff reported that on the group's two prior trips to Washington, D. C., a year earlier, the members were very excited, felt important, and expressed a desire to return. One year later the same youths were no longer interested in going to Washington.

Ethnic Identity Phase

On the basis of the analysis quoted earlier, in the fall of 1965, an attempt was made to reconstitute a small group. The Negro staff member was hired full-time as the only staff. The emphasis for the first six months was on Negro cultural identity. (Puerto Ricans and other whites were never excluded from the group, and some would drop in once or twice but never became members.) The worker stimulated a series of discussions and invited Negro guest speakers to address the group on community problems as well as the arts, theater, etc. The members went as a group to hear Dr. Martin Luther King at a rally on South African racism. They at-

[3] One hypothesis was that in 1964, when MFY was publicly attacked by the *Daily News,* the agency for a period of weeks restrained the Young Adult Action Group from picketing the *News,* thereby lessening the commitment of the members to Mobilization and increasing their sense of impotence.

tended plays depicting Negro history and culture. The discussions
were often set up in the form of debates.

During these debates and discussions there were about twenty
members who attended consistently. Of these twenty, five or six
were verbal, and the rest listened. There was no pressure from the
worker to get anyone to speak. An observer of these meetings reported that some members came for months without saying a
word during the discussions. The draft, integration, Vietnam, the
Black Muslims, and black separatism were among the topics discussed, as well as more general subjects such as the history of
slavery, the emerging African nations, and the South today.

One side effect of these discussions was that the members got
to know each other very well. It became apparent to them that they
did not all think alike, nor did they all agree with the worker,
who did not hide his opinions from the group. Mobilization, a
white-dominated agency, was often a target of attack—a symbol
of the Establishment whenever the agency rules or policies con-
flicted with the desires of the group regarding such matters as
drinking or political affiliation. Although the worker and some
members of the group at times protested loudly against the sponsoring agency, the members' need for the Young Adult Action
Group and, therefore, for the financial and structural support of
MFY was overriding.[4]

Programmatic ideas were introduced by having discussions of
various community problems. After a series of these discussions,
the group voted on a single issue around which to plan program—
police brutality. Many of the members had been in trouble with
the law, and some had experienced police intimidation and har-
assment. There were also members, however, who had never had
any trouble with the police.

The group held a community rally on police brutality which was
attended by approximately 250 neighborhood teen-agers. Follow-

[4] In disagreement with the Young Adult Action Group over policy, such
as joining a coalition with politically partisan organizations, MFY insisted
only that the group, through its staff worker, be made aware of all the
ramifications of its actions to MFY and to itself. From 1965 onward the
agency allowed the group to do anything that was legal.

ing the rally, they picketed the 9th Precinct for alleged police brutality inflicted on three local Puerto Rican girls. This picketing led to several meetings of the Young Adult Action Group attended by police community-relations officers, as well as to an advertising campaign in the community, advising all teen-agers who had problems with the police to come to the group for help. Very few actually came.[5]

The organization was at its high point during this period in early 1966. It is difficult to determine precisely why. On the one hand the emphasis on ethnic history and identity seemed to strengthen the group. Erikson's ideas seemed to be corroborated:

> Adolescent development comprises a new set of identification processes, both with significant persons and with ideological forces, which give importance to individual life by relating it to a living community and to ongoing history, and by counterpointing the newly won individual identity with some communal solidarity. . . . To enter history each generation of young persons must find an identity consonant with its own childhood and consonant with an ideological promise in the perceptible historical process. . . .[6]

On a more functional level, the planned cultural programs available every week were a distinct attraction. As will be noted, karate also stabilized the attendance. In addition, though the group had its highest number of active participants during this period, its involvement with social action was not high. Police brutality was the only program.

Because the staff worker who hypothesized the need for ethnic identification as a precursor to social action left after being with the group less than nine months, there was not enough time for a real test of his ideas. The new worker was not so committed to this point of view.

[5] It is unclear why. Perhaps teen-agers were frightened, or perhaps police brutality is not so rampant as believed. Also a new staff worker had taken over at this point. His skills lay in agitating, not in following up on day-to-day details, verifying incidents, developing communication, etc.

[6] Erik Erikson, "Youth: Fidelity and Diversity," *The Challenge of Youth,* Erik Erikson, editor (New York, Doubleday Anchor Books, 1965), p. 24.

Social-Service Phase

During an evaluation of the growth and development of the Young Adult Action Group at this time, several conclusions emerged. First, the more direct the connection between a project and the members' daily lives, the more interest and commitment were put into the project. Second, when projects are related to the adult community, members will assume a great deal of responsibility and initiative if they are permitted to perform adult roles. A striking example of this phenomenon occurred in a Head Start program which employed Neighborhood Youth Corps workers. Two groups members were employed in this program in the summer of 1966. Their supervisor told the group worker that these boys were disinterested, irresponsible, and unable to perform the duties assigned to them (these duties were similar to the traditional junior-counselor duties in a camp). After some consultation, the two members were given the sole responsibility for organizing a meeting of the parents of the Head Start children. These two Young Adult Action Group members, on their own initiative and through their own means, got 85 percent of the parents to attend the meeting which they organized. This attendance was quite spectacular and about double that secured in any other meeting organized by Head Start in the area.

The major issue of concern during this evaluation was the lack of social-action projects. The constant pumping in of projects by the staff was viewed as a sign of weakness in the organization. Some contended that a forceful staff programmatic role is inherently unsuited to a youth-action group. They argued that the presence of a staff worker who constantly prods members into action, undermines the need for commitment and responsibility on the part of the members, and inevitably leads to problem definition and solution in adult and professional terms. Others, granting the essential validity of this point of view, nevertheless wondered what kind of program would develop a vibrant organization. They pointed to the fact that when staff had not suggested programs, the programs had not been forthcoming from the youths.

The criteria for project success noted above—adult recognition, relatedness to adolescent life, and tangible results—suggested that independently conceived programs might develop out of the experience of the group's members' staffing and organizing their own adolescent service center, a place where teen-agers could help other teen-agers in trouble. Such a program would constantly put them in contact with adult, professional, and lay people, would be directly related to the problems of teen-agers on the Lower East Side, and would offer tangible manifestations of success and failure: Did a client get a job, get out of jail, is he still sick, etc.

Without abandoning the emphasis on cultural identity, in the fall of 1966 the Young Adult Action Group pinned its theoretical hopes on ideas about youth involvement.

> The concept of youth involvement can be an essential step leading to the growth and development of responsible adults. . . . Generically "youth involvement" refers to varying sets of procedures that can be employed to enable youth to participate directly in the activities, programs, services, etc., that are designed to affect them. . . . If a youth-development or delinquency project has some kind of change as its ultimate objective, then it is the youth target group of the project who are at once both the objects and agents of change. . . . In these projects, it is the context of the project itself, rather than the service being dispensed, that provides the incentives for change. Included here are opportunities for enchanced understanding of the self, opportunities for participation in decision making and problem solving of various kinds, opportunities to become a man or woman through participation in some continuing, consistent, and socially sanctioned enterprise. . . . The basis for the youth-involvement approach lies in our knowledge of the overwhelming significance of psychosocial development during the adolescent years, the role of "identity" in determining behavior and behavioral change, and the role of the social structure in shaping, frustrating and enhancing them.[7]

It was hoped that through working with the problems of local youth, Young Adult Action Group members would become aware of the institutional barriers and inadequacies in community re-

[7] June Shmelzer, "Youth Involvement: A Position Paper" (mimeographed, Washington, D.C., Department of Health, Education and Welfare, October, 1966).

sources. Thus, needed programs and projects should be obvious from the individual problems brought to the group's adolescent service center. For example, the difficulty of finding employment for older adolescents, even after they have attended training programs, might be translated into a social-action campaign to break down barriers to employment and admission to various unions. Problems presented by narcotic addicts could be translated into social-atcion demand for specific rehabilitation programs. Problems brought to the center in relation to the courts and the legal system could lead to demands for statutory revisions. It was also hoped that the group's adolescent service center would ultimately teach youngsters an array of possible tactics for solving community problems which could go beyond limited protest demonstrations.

Program and attendance had dropped off during the summer, so the early fall of 1966 was used to recruit members and reinstitute the Negro culture and history focus. A teacher of Negro history was hired who gave talks and led disscussions each week prior to the business meeting of the Young Adult Action Group. The group also sponsored a karate class which was very popular. Attendance averaged around fifteen at the regular meetings. In early January 1967 the organization hired four of its own members to staff its storefront adolescent service center.

At this point a series of administrative difficulties developed. The staff worker resigned, and an appropriate replacement could not be found for several months. The caseworker hired to supervise the adolescent service center was unable to organize a coherent training program for the group caseworkers. Attendance at meetings was sporadic. The organization was on the verge of disintegration.

It was late spring before the adolescent service center began operating.[8] With the advent of summer 90 percent of all requests for service were for jobs. This suggested the possibility of mounting a social-action program to demand the continuation through the fall of summer jobs provided by the Neighborhood Youth Corps. Well over a thousand teen-agers were contacted through

8 The chapter on "Adolescent Service Centers" in this volume describes some of the casework activities of the adolescent workers in this center.

group meetings at various Neighborhood Youth Corps work sites on the Lower East Side, and a large rally was held at City Hall in September in conjunction with other groups around the city. Poor staff planning resulted in some disorder at the picket line and in an inability to maintain the campaign after the initial rally. By October it was clear that the group would be terminated in December because of a cutback in funds. This demoralized the few remaining members, although the organization participated in a conference in Washington in support of a juvenile-delinquency bill and continued to operate the adolescent service center.[9]

Conclusion

The idea of developing social action out of a social service was not given an adequate test in the Young Adult Action Group, nor was the conception that the commitment required for social action must be rooted in a secure personal identity. There are nevertheless a number of conclusions that can be drawn from the experience.

The goal of having the youth develop their own social-action programs was unrealistic without first giving youth exposure to and experience with varying perspectives on the social milieu in which they lived. It is not accidental that in all societies it is a segment of the university youth who are social actionists. They are exposed to broad perspectives and aware of their options. The adolescent service center might have provided some of this needed perspective.[10]

The idea that youth can be converted en masse from delinquency to social action seems overoptimistic. The often-cited correlation of a decrease in delinquency with a rise in civil-rights activity in Birmingham postulates a condition which has not been present in such areas as the Lower East Side. In Birmingham, almost the

[9] A very useful training session for the Young Adult Action Group caseworkers was finally organized in the fall; all the participants voiced approval of these sessions.

[10] The plan was to have the adolescent service workers summarize their caseloads biweekly at the Young Adult Action Group meetings in order to get the thinking of the membership on possible social-action programs which might help solve some of the individual problems.

entire Negro adult community was involved and aroused at the bus incident involving Mrs. Parks. Such widespread involvement has seldom been the case in the North. Further, the internal control maintained by the adult Negro community was extremely powerful in Birmingham at this time; it certainly played a considerable part in lessening delinquency.

The Negro community, like every other ethnic community, is itself stratified, and this stratification is manifiested in the community's organizations. The Young Adult Action Group experience shows that a social-action organization, like any other group, tends to become associated with a given clique. In the action group, the rough members pulled out and for a time made the organization the target of their delinquency. The problem of creating an organization that can recruit and maintain the participation of rougher elements still remains to be solved. The karate class seems to have been of use toward this end—some former dissidents did return. Yet it is unlikely that diverse groups can be maintained in one organization.[11]

If social action is to be the major program of a teen-agers' organization, then tie-ins with larger social-action structures are necessary for program stimulation. The group was initially fed programs by the civil-rights movement; when the movement waned, the organization waned.

A social-action organization requires a good deal of emotional intensity and independence to be successful. It remains to be seen if a social agency supported by public funds can tolerate the kinds of activity this emotional intensity engenders. Mobilization often had to walk a tightrope during the last four years, falling back on the legalism that the Young Adult Action Group was free to make its own decisions as long as they were not illegal but that MFY had the right to dissociate itself from these decisions. The situation was problematic in that the organization was to a great extent under the control of the staff person, no matter what or who

[11] A suggestion was made to use the Young Adult Action Group to interest other teen-age groups in carrying out social action in their own organization and under their own auspices. This strategy did not work in MFY's voter-registration campaigns. See the chapter on "Voter Registration Campaigns" in Vol. 2, *Community Development*.

that staff person was. (The problem of stability without the worker has not been solved.) Thus the agency knows that it is vulnerable. If it controls too little, its own stability may be threatened; if it controls too much, its social-action aim may be destroyed.

Finally, a problem related to the lodging of social-action organization in social agencies is the assumption that the development of true identity will lead a youth to social action. It may be that such a youth will instead take the path of education, middle-class aspiration, and involvement with the formidable task of taking advantage of the opportunities already opened up to him. Nevertheless, it is important that social agencies aid Negro youths in the process of identifying with their ethnic background by providing opportunities for expressing that identity—social action being one of those opportunities, cultural arts and education being others. Social agencies should provide a variety of such programs.

11

Adolescent Service Centers

Beverly Luther and Harold H. Weissman

It is unlikely that changes can be brought about in gang behavior and attitudes unless commensurate changes are made in the social situation that breeds the gang. Although this fact has long been known to social agencies, they have lacked the resources to affect social situations. Their efforts have therefore been confined to a variety of programs designed to influence the gang directly. Mobilization's experience with several such programs, reported in the preceding papers, lends credence to the view that the gang or peer group should not be the major target of programs designed to lessen the incidence of juvenile delinquency. The Mobilization experience seems to suggest that delinquent gang groupings must be broken up, but not without providing a new set of social conditions which support the transition of gang members into more acceptable roles. Previous papers have noted that the systematic subjugation of fighting gangs in the late 1950's and early 1960's resulted not only in the breakup of the gangs but also in the addiction of thousands of former participants. At that time a new social situation or set of conditions was not provided.

A major target of programs for delinquents should be the way in which institutions in a neighborhood are related to adolescents. If these institutions are made to work effectively for delinquents, it is likely that there will be effects on the existing gang structure.[1]

---

[1] To break down a gang's structure quickly, one must also attack its internal functioning. Thus a detached worker, instead of trying to use the group to harness group support for changing various attitudes and values

In the fall of 1965, Lower East Side settlement houses undertook an intensive evaluation of their detached worker programs. Several facts emerged: (1) The worker's time was being spent not with the gang or group as a whole but with individual members, meeting individual problems related to school, jobs, police, etc. (2) Attempts to bring delinquents into regular settlement house programs were not successful, and groups which had been brought into the settlements did not exhibit a marked diminution of delinquent acts outside the settlement. (3) Once gang fighting had subsided, continuing to work with the gang in relation to group activity in many ways preserved the existence of the gang.

The experience of the Mobilization coffee-shop program (1963–65) seemed to indicate that the older adolescent in particular needed help with his individual problems of work, social relationships, school, etc. The coffee shops failed for many reasons, [2] but they demonstrated that teen-agers had an overwhelming need for a place and a person to come to with their personal problems. As this idea developed and the structural limitations of the coffee shops as a device to meet the need became apparent, it was hoped that Mobilization's neighborhood service centers could provide the kind of help needed by the area's youth population. This hope did not materialize. Although the neighborhood service centers were designed to provide a broad range of services in an informal, personal, and nonbureaucratic manner, the percentage of teen-age clients among the applicants was miniscule. Referrals from the coffee shops were not successful, and few teen-agers returned after an initial visit. Apparently the centers were regarded by teen-agers as organizations operated by and for adults. The staff were not accustomed to working with teen-agers, especially low-income teen-agers, who presented problems that required special approaches, resources, and solutions. And finally, it was apparent that there was a lack of consensus in the casework field as to how

---

of the gang members, might attempt to break down the group by constantly relating the members to new conditions in the neighborhood, such as new school or work programs. In slum areas where delinquency is rampant, the existing gang groupings without question support delinquent behavior.

[2] See the chapter on "Group Service Programs and Their Effect on Delinquents" in this volume.

to give individual help to low-income youth. A recent article summed this up as follows:

> Studies of the use of the casework method with delinquents have generally been disappointing. Casework procedures as reported in *Girls at Vocational High* did not produce noteworthy results. Also, the services studied by Tate and Hodges did not furnish evidence of success for such methods and one of the pioneer works in the field—the Cambridge Summerville Study—indicated that over two-thirds of the boys who were involved in the experiment failed to benefit from the services offered. There is sufficient evidence to warrant the conclusion that the efficacy of preventive casework is not demonstrated in these projects.[3]

The situation in 1965, then, was that the detached workers of the five settlement houses were serving only two hundred known gang members (a very small percentage of the troubled youth in the Mobilization area); the coffee shops were closed; the neighborhood service centers were regarded as belonging to the adults; and the settlement houses and community centers had no programs for the nonaffiliated teen-agers of the community.

MFY therefore decided to offer the adolescent his own service center, where he would be guaranteed an interested adult who would provide immediate help with his presenting problem and guidance through the various institutions and bureaucracies geared to deal with his other problems. The first center designed to test the efficacy of this approach was operated by Mobilization itself.

The MFY adolescent service center (ASC) was located in a storefront, with a waiting room and a reception desk in front and three cubbyhole offices in the back. In the waiting room were chairs, magazines, and a coffee pot. There were two full-time male workers and one part-time female worker. All three of the staff had had considerable experience working with low-income teen-agers. One of the male workers was Puerto Rican.

Before it opened, the center did a lot of advertising. Posters were displayed around the neighborhood announcing the wares to be dispensed: "HELP WITH SCHOOL," "JOBS," "ADDIC-

[3] William P. Lentz, "Delinquency as a Stable Role," *Social Work*, (October 1966), p. 66.

TION," "LEGAL AID." Flyers were printed and stuffed in mailboxes of the tenements and public housing in the neighborhood. Wallet-size cards giving the name, address, and telephone number of the center were distributed. Schools, settlement houses, police precincts, and probation and parole offices were notified of the service. The target population was any and all teen-agers in the area with any and all problems.

Teen-agers did come, a few at a time in the beginning. As word spread, intake reached a steady sixty per month. By the end of the eighth month of service, half of the adolescent-service-center clients were self-referred, having been told of the center by other clients.

Several important facts were learned from this first ASC. It became clear that most teen-agers' presenting problem was only one item from a long list of interrelated difficulties, including poor health, suspension from school, truancy, difficulty with probation, destructive home environment, basic inadequacies in educational preparation, etc. A large percentage of the older group presented crisis situations which had to be handled immediately if they were not to further impair individual functioning and hope for the future. Again, the mere existence of a place to which teen-agers could go for help and general support was invaluable. Many of the clients represented a segment of the population that was adrift, with no attachment to family, school, settlement house, or any other organized institution of society. There was no question that the adolescent service center met a serious need of the adolescent population.

When Mobilization in 1966 asked the settlement houses to shift from the concept of providing detached workers to deal with gangs to running adolescent service centers, there was a mixed reaction. Although all the workers involved had been giving individualized service to gang members, and actually had helped to promote the Mobilization adolescent service center, they were nevertheless reluctant to give up the gang. Most of them were trained group workers and had faith in their techniques, which require the existence of a group to be practiced.[4]

[4] Anyone who has worked with youths or adults during severe crises will recognize how difficult it is not to become involved in the secondary grati-

The adolescent-service-center concept was sanctioning the breakup of gangs when it stipulated that the centers were not to be hangouts for any one group of teen-agers. There were to be no recreation facilities, pool tables, ping-pong tables, etc. The rationale for this rule was that if any center became known as the turf of a particular gang, the nongang members would not feel comfortable using it. In actuality, the original client group of the MFY center were gang members with whom workers had developed a relationship. In most cases, the worker interpreted the center policy of no-hanging-around effectively, and the gang members were served individually like everyone else. The five agencies receiving detached-worker contracts for 1966–67 agreed to set up adolescent service centers in storefronts outside their agency which would follow the general procedures and policies of the MFY center.[5]

By May 1967, all of the ASC's had the following in common: (1) Over one third of each center's intake represented teen-agers who never went to the parent settlement house for any of its programs and had never been involved in the detached-worker programs. This figure substantiated the assumption that settlement houses often take on an image which is rejected by large numbers of low-income youths. Thus, the adolescent service centers represent an important adjunct to the local settlement houses. (2) The teen-age clients were receptive to the service they received. Although there was some variation among centers, one agency's records indicate that 90% of the follow-up appointments were kept after the initial contact. Given the disappointing rate of broken appointments by teen-agers at the neighborhood service centers, this is an

---

fication of "working with danger"—of mixing with a population that the general public is afraid of, be it delinquents, criminals, mental patients, etc. This gratification is usually unconscious but is continually fed by an admiring public—girl friend, wife, classmate, fellow workers. It is not nearly so glamorous to say, "I work in an adolescent service center," as to say, "I work with the Henry Street Dukes, the Untouchables, the Forsythe Street Boys, the Comanches, the Imperial Dragons. . . ."

[5] In this instance Mobilization was successful in its institutional-change efforts. Not only did a new program develop out of prior experience, but this new program represented a dramatic shift in policy.

extremely significant statistic. (3) Each center served its immediate neighborhood, was open during the critical hours of teen mobility (after school and evenings), and operated with a high degree of informality and accessibility. Clients would always be seen, with or without an appointment. (4) Although the adolescent service centers were not conceived of as job centers, about two thirds of the requests for service were in the job area. The other third was divided among school, medical, legal, narcotic, and family problems.

Grand Street Settlement was the first settlement to operate an adolescent service center. This facility was housed in the community center of the housing project where most of the settlement's clients lived. An excerpt from the final eighteen-month evaluation of this center is illustrative of the work done in the adolescent service centers.

We began with finding jobs and offering help with legal and medical problems. Finding jobs for boys and girls was a popular selling point of the center. . . . Old teens who were helped sent their friends, and the center reached out and offered help in finding jobs in spite of the fact that we were not sure we could produce. No promises or guarantees were ever made. Only to listen and honestly try to help, this was the agreement. . . .

As the center built its reputation and proved its respect for teens, a few at a time began to share their more personal needs. Thus we began counseling, taking teens to court, helping them find lawyers, taking and referring drug-dependent youths to hospitals.

In the beginning, there were few in-school clients. However, with our initiating a relationship with Seward Park High School and speaking with the graduating senior classes and providing help and guidance in finding decent jobs, the flood gates were opened to high school students who needed all kinds of help.

For students, the center offered tutorial service, help with other school problems, such as conferences with teachers, guidance counselors, job counselors and principals, depending on the area of the problem.

In numbers of "problem areas," both short-term and counseling in depth were carried on. . . .

A breakdown of problem areas into percentages looks as follows:

60%   Jobs
15%   Tutorial Program
10%   Counseling Cases
5%   Medical Referrals
5%   School/Education Problems
5%   Legal/Court

Adults within the community were not formally organized as a committee, but worked as individuals on . . . job finding in the community and helping to advertise the center's services through direct contact with teenagers.

Adults from outside the community were used as tutors to help interested teens, both junior high and high school, to improve their marks and reading ability. Various subjects were taught, such as mathematics, geometry, English reading, and Spanish.

. . . I think the idea of an adolescent service center is a good one. If the center were to continue, I would use teens in the capacity of receptionists and assistants in the routine work. They can be trained to do much of the follow-up, telephoning for jobs, etc. . . . Indigenous youth have . . . a kind of relationship to the teen community that no adult worker can expect to have. . . . They often know immediately who needs help because they know the youths.[6]

The center should be accessible to the . . . teen population, or at least located on a site that allows teens to comfortably drop in. However . . . this does not have to be a major selling point—it is . . . making good your commodity that sells the center. Services

---

[6] In the adolescent service center described in the chapter "Negro Youth and Social Action" in this volume, an attempt was made to use adolescents as counselors. This experiment was hampered by staff's inability to mount a successful training program for the adolescent counselors. Two months before this project terminated, a well-organized training program was put into effect, but because of the limited time period the full effect of training could not be gauged. An observer made the following comment: "The general quality of service did not improve; certain . . . perceptions persisted, such as the notion that 'giving help' in the professional sense was equivalent to coddling and that empathy involved a diminution of manhood (or selfhood). There were some encouraging signs after training: a growth of awareness that there are learnable, affectively neutral techniques one can employ in dealing with people; that there are instances where one's ego can be separated from one's response; and that there are many clues available from an individual's demeanor about his attitude. And lastly, each worker was made a little more conscious of his particular assets and shortcomings as a 'service-giving person'."

and resources should be determined by the needs of the teens you hope to serve.

The use of local-community adults in direct contacts with teens of the neighborhood was emphasized in the center operated by Educational Alliance. When the storefront opened, the merchants on the street were highly skeptical, if not outright hostile. By the end of the year they were volunteering to man the storefront if the worker had to go out, training teens in their own stores, canvassing the neighborhood for jobs, and just dropping in to talk to the youngsters or the staff. Through direct contact, a see-for-yourself approach, the merchants were given a chance to see the problem from the teen-ager's point of view.[7]

Group-counseling sessions were never formally organized in any of the centers except Mobilization's. It was felt that a center would have to be in operation for a year before establishing formal counseling groups, so that staff could get to know the clients and place them in the appropriate groups. The staff of the settlement adolescent service centers also stated that they were too busy meeting individual needs and adjusting to the new service to spend time organizing formal groups. Groups did meet informally, when the need arose, at both the Educational Alliance and Grand Street settlements. Mobilization's experience in grouping teen-agers with similar problems was not successful.

The use of formal group counseling, which demands a time commitment, verbalization skill, and long-range planning, may be difficult for this teen-age population. Certainly more precise methods of group selection, timing of referrals, etc., are required.[8] The prime motivation of those using the centers was their need for help with an immediate problem. The worker could maintain contact with the client only if the relationship was defined as "I'm

[7] This concept was based on the idea that delinquency is a community problem and that social workers should not be the buffers between the adult community and delinquents. It also differed from the traditional adult-youth council in that adults were not asked to come and plan with or for adolescents. They were asked to provide services—tutoring, jobs, a place to sleep, etc.

[8] See the chapter on "Vocational Counseling" in Vol. 3, *Employment and Educational Services,* for a description of a successful group-counseling experiment.

here when you need me." Successful referral for group counseling probably must wait until the client has tested this relationship and found it to be true.

Conclusion

The adolescent service center proved to be an effective mechanism for reaching a large number of adolescents with problems who were not being served by traditional programs in settlement houses. The visibility and accessibility of the service centers were important ingredients in their success in attracting teen-agers. Although the service strategy involved working with individuals, it was necessary for workers to maintain their relationships with gangs and other such groupings.

An adolescent service center can serve as a kind of first-aid station, handling crisis situations. It can serve as a bridge between the client and various institutional resources, as an extension of its role as a referral agency. The workers can be equipped to act as coordinators, negotiators, and advocates. The center can serve as a counseling service on both a group and an individual basis. It can serve as an ancillary treatment center for the other agencies which carry the major responsibility for a client; for example, a center can operate in conjunction with schools in remedial tutoring or guidance, it can work with hospitals in prenatal care and parent education, and it can work with the courts. Finally, an adolescent service center can serve as a base for community participation in solving the problems of delinquency. This can be accomplished not only through discussions and planning committees but, more significantly, by providing opportunities for adults to help teen-agers.

Despite the teen-agers' acceptance of the adolescent service centers, the results to date indicate only limited success in dealing with the problems presented. New techniques need to be developed to deal with unemployment, poor education, addiction, and various other problems. One technique which certainly deserves attention is the concept of youth involvement in operation of the centers. Another is related to methods of organizing group counseling. The ultimate success of adolescent service centers will depend on the ability of such institutions as the schools, employment services, and the courts to adapt themselves successfully to the low-income adolescent. The adolescent service center has a role to play in shaping the adaptation of these institutions and in helping adolescents to avail themselves of any new opportunity offered. Finally, an adolescent service center may be regarded as a kind of anchor for a great many slum youths who without it might drift into social and personal destructiveness. The middle-class youth has his family and society's institutions, which he understands and which by and large understand him, to cushion his mistakes and shocks during the maturation process. Lower-class young men and women, lacking a resourceful family and alienated from such institutions as school and church, also need time to grow up. The adolescent service centers give such adolescents the time they require.

12

Training Youth in the Arts

Henry Heifetz

One of the goals of the coffee-shop program, discussed in an earlier paper in this section was the development of artistic skills among Lower East Side young people. However, the shops accomplished little along these lines. There were programs in the fine arts and in photography, museum and gallery trips were arranged for small groups, and a choral group was formed. The theater program succeeded in presenting a play, *Dope,* in which major roles were enacted by youngsters who themselves had been or were involved with drugs. A summer-theater program was conducted in which *Dope* and other plays were given a few performances in public. However, the facilities at the coffee shops were inadequate for effective programs of this nature.

In the spring of 1965, with the demise of the coffee-house program, funds became available for a training program in the arts. The projected Cultural Arts Program, although intended to provide youth with opportunities to develop their artistic talents, had a much broader goal as well—to enhance the self-esteem of slum youth. The focus of attack was to be the symbols by which youth develop their identity and sense of self-esteem—and ultimately their sense of what opportunities in life they will take advantage of. Cultural themes and material would be emphasized.

A work-training program was set up in four divisions of the arts. Trainees were to put in twenty hours per week for a stipend of $25. (The training time has since been reduced to sixteen hours and the stipend to $20.) The divisions were modern dance, drama (including a film-making group), fine arts, and choral music. A professional theater director was hired to head the Cultural Arts Program, and he in turn selected four specialists and four assistants to conduct the training sessions. In November 1965 the program began with an enrollment of thirty-three teen-agers between the ages of sixteen and twenty-one, all residents of the Lower East Side and members of low-income families. Their suitability for the program had been determined on the basis of samples of their work and interviews. The objectives of the program were (1) to provide opportunities for talented adolescents in the community to develop their artistic abilities in a professional setting and to give them some basis for realizing their career aspirations, (2) to dramatize the underutilization of the natural artistic abilities of low-income minority group youths and the need for locally based quality-art facilities for youth, and (3) to give minority-group youths a greater sense of pride and self-worth through knowledge of, training in, and expression of their cultural heritage, using the various art forms. The wish was also expressed to achieve a greater sense of community by developing a cultural-arts and education program in which the neighborhood will take pride.

Classical and Folk Culture

Of the four divisions of the Cultural Arts Program, choral music training was probably the most closely related to the Western classical tradition of art, emphasizing a traditionally "beautiful" style and the classical works which are the most thorough test of this style.

Six boys and a girl sit in a semicircle around the choral instructor who is at the piano. The arrangement winds from deep voices on the far left to the highest voices on the right, and includes three Negroes, two Puerto Ricans, one Chinese, and a Jewish girl. They are repeating a couple of bars in parts and then together, separately if the instructor hears some mistake or fault in the voice, and then together again, sometimes to the instructor's piano accompaniment, sometimes without it, patiently, not objecting to the continual repetition until the close harmony seems right and the instructor is satisfied. The instructor is friendly but thorough, exacting, and professional in his manner.

A boy relatively new to the group, a Puerto Rican about seventeen with a high, clear tenor voice, is told that he needs . . . greater projection and control of breathing and that the instructor will work with him separately later. The instructor passes out part music for the Hallelujah Chorus of Handel's *Messiah* and tells them to turn to a particular page. . . . A tall Negro boy . . . says to his friend, "Man, I'm so sick of this song. Like, that's all we did last Friday, this song." A few minutes later he and the Puerto Rican tenor are practicing a short section of the chorus over and over again, with interest and gradual improvement, as the instructor tells them that this kind of music, with its long continuous line, requires very consistent, careful breath control, and then shows them how it's done.

The question comes up in the choral-music division, but just as importantly in the others, of the relationship between the traditional fine arts and the life and culture of the ghetto poor. True folk culture—basically feeding upon its own traditions, dependent mainly on live performance and oral transmission—is becoming more and more of a rarity throughout the world. Even in many underdeveloped societies, where the artistic culture of the poor remains basically a folk culture, it is frequently subject, in this era of rapid comunications, to the influence of the pop culture transmitted by the mass media. An influenced folk culture of this kind continues to exist in some of the more underdeveloped rural areas of the United States, but the major artistic influences in an urban slum are those of a ghettoized commercial culture. Spanish popular music, black "soul" music, certain verbal traditions of joking and "sounding" and protective slang, the styles of dance favored by Puerto Rican or Negro youngsters—these are the artistic materials with which the Cultural Arts Program sought to make connections, in order to feed the trainees out of their own environment, to give them sources of power for the development of original rather than imitative talent.

The program laid a great deal of emphasis on this idea of roots, particularly in the choice of material. The drama group put on public performances in which the life styles of the Lower East

Side were accepted and presented as the natural background for statement, reminiscent in a way of the Group Theater of the thirties. In fact, one of the Group Theater's best-known plays, Odets' *Waiting for Lefty*, was sucessfully presented in a comtemporary adaptation revolving around the issue of rent strikes on the Lower East Side.

Although all the Cultural Arts divisions concerned themselves with broad ethnic awareness, it was probably within the most abstract of them, the dance, that this element came out most strongly.

The dance company of the Cultural Arts Program is presenting a concert of works choreographed by the participants themselves. The concert is held in a studio in the twenties before a small audience. There are five numbers, two to African drum rhythms played by the instructor, one to a Miriam Makeba African song, one to electronic music, one a talk-dance with no accompaniment but bits of dialogue which three girls shout and interpret in movement together with some off-stage shouted words from other members of the company. The dance movements are strong, angry, modern. There are seven members of the company, three boys and four girls, all Negro. There is a dance with sticks which suggests African ritual dancing and one in street clothes (otherwise they wear black leotards) which has somewhat of the mood of Genet's play *The Blacks*, dancers opposed to audience, somewhat mocking, dancing a sudden minuet for a moment out of brusque walking and running movements, concluding with a fixed stare at the audience and a breakup into loud laughter. There is a final quintet to electronic music with much modern reaching out and rejection and pursuit and imaged suffering between man and woman. The kids have not been perfect, there have been movements which didn't come off, some steps and gestures which were clearly meant to be simultaneous on the part of two dancers and were not, but they have been moving and strong, with a great deal of stage presence. After the final number they sit down tired in the dancing space, seven young bodies, and answer questions about their dances.

Notwithstanding the emphasis on local culture, the trainees were being groomed for possible professional accomplishment in the arts, which meant that primary attention was given, not to the development of a folk culture, but to the perfecting of professional skills. A description of an art exhibit illustrates this:

> An exhibition of the work of the art program is opening tonight. Under the direction of the instructor and his assistant, the trainees are cleaning up the rooms, painting the walls white, attaching thick brown paper to those parts of the walls where drawings are to be stapled. The exhibition will be open for a couple of weeks. The trainees joke about having preferred positions for their paintings and drawings. The instructor talks with the kids about what should be exhibited and what shouldn't, emphasizing that only the best things should go up. They begin hanging the paintings. They are paintings of forms and people; the stress in this program is on basics, on drawing, on color, on development of the essential tools. A couple of paintings, of simple interiors, show an impressive feeling for gradations of color, and the instructor points out the artist, a tall Puerto Rican boy.
>
> Some of the other paintings and many of the drawings show considerable talent but two paintings especially, a still life and a portrait of a thin, dark, lonely-looking girl, stand out. They tend toward expressionism and are highly colored and agitated. The instructor says the girl who did them is the best in his program. She has won a scholarship to art school for next year. The girl arrives a bit later, carrying a sheaf of drawings. She is a dark-skinned Puerto Rican, about seventeen, small, poorly dressed, awkward in her movements, and shy. She produces a couple of large drawings that seem even better than the paintings, one of herself drawn in with strong lines against a background of two hanging frying pans arranged asymetrically, her face brooding and sad. The instructor says that when she came into the program she could barely draw a tabletop.

Art and Opportunity

Very few opportunities are available for artistically talented youngsters among the poor to get serious professional instruction. The Cultural Arts Program tried to give the trainees a reservoir of vital artistic skills and to develop their capacity to make use of these skills originally, in drawing, painting, dancing, or dramatic improvisations. In view of the fact that most of these trainees go to school or hold full-time jobs, the amount of time they devote to the arts program—sixteen hours per week—is considerable and taxing. Certainly not all will go on to make professions of the arts, but the possibility is there. And beyond that possibility, there is the simple knowledge that their awareness of things and capacity to express their judgments and feelings about them are expanding, that the roof of a tenement is not the only open place in life.

Despite the narrowness and the overriding economic restriction of ghetto life, young men and women from minority-group backgrounds, once they are given access to the necesary knowledge, have many assets to bring to their pursuit of the arts. They come from groups that emphasize emotion and expression far more than middle-class America does, and they can draw on this background for their art, music, dance, and drama. There is also the fact that this is a period when many more opportunities are open in the performing arts for Negro and Puerto Rican performers than was once the case.[2]

In the relatively short time that the Cultural Arts Program has been in existence, there have already been a certain number of professional placements. Two trainees have gone on to prepare to teach dance and two to teach drama. Two are acting in films and on the stage, one singer has a contract with a record company, and several art students have had their work exhibited in small professional galleries. Others have won scholarships for advanced study. At its most immediate level, the program has proved to be a valuable stepping stone for individual talented youth. But there have been other, broader gains as well.

Arts and the Audience

One of the twenty-two street performances put on by the drama program in the summer of 1966 is in progress on a Lower East Side street, on a temporary stage. It is a warm, clear New York night. The crowd is large, mostly Puerto Rican, in T-shirts and open cotton shirts, light dresses and slacks. They are watching the performance of an adapted version of *Waiting for Lefty,* dealing with

[2] Nevertheless, the performing arts at this point in time cannot be considered as a major source of employment for minority groups.

Lower East Side rent strikes. A group of teen-age Puerto Rican kids watch intently, and a Vista worker, attached to the Cultural Arts Program, happens to place himself near them. A fight scene breaks out on stage, with actors spilling around, banging objects, crashing down. The kids react excitedly, cheering and taking sides. "Jus' like real," they say, "jus' like real."

Aside from the effects of the Cultural Arts Program on the participating trainees, another point to be considered is that of its usefulness in relation to the Lower East Side community as a whole. The performing groups—chorus, dance, drama—have put on a number of free public performances in the streets of the neighborhood, with programs shaped to Lower East Side interests and problems. The drama group especially has concerned itself from the outset with plays and films very close in content to the social problems of the community. A public performance of the play *Dope* has been filmed, as has a story written and directed by a seventeen-year-old black trainee, with the actors and technicians all members of the program. The film, called *You Dig It,* about gang warfare on the Lower East Side, won a local film competition, and another film, *The Game,* about the cycle of entrapments in the slum, won first prize, documentary class, in the 1967 Venice Film Festival.

The presentation of such films and the public production of socially conscious drama on the Lower East Side are useful in two ways. Most immediately, they serve as educative influences by calling attention to the problems and underlining possibilities for solutions. In addition, effective drama involves the spectators in the action and judgments. And, as a result, something more might be hoped for than the merely educative. It is possible that greater awareness and pride in the best of minority-group values might spread outward, from the performers back to the community from which they were derived.

The audiences at the public performances held during the summer of 1966 and 1967 were generally quite large. Earlier performances sometimes had to deal with hostile or contemptuous spectators, especially teen-agers, who made so much noise that it became difficult for the performers to continue. Such disturbances eventually disappeared, and there were even instances when hecklers in the audience were controlled by other spectators, who wanted to see and hear what was being done. The interest on the Lower East Side in these summer performances is already considerable. It would seem that, with the proper plays, the interrelation can be very rewarding for the young performers who have a sympathetic local audience and the people of the Lower East Side who come for entertainment and may find a little bit more.

Currently there are about fifty youngsters participating in the MFY Cultural Arts Program. Most of them would have had little chance to develop in their art were it not for the activity. When one considers not only the importance it has had for its participants but also the interest such activities as the summer theater have generated in the neighborhood, the program becomes even more impressive, despite its relatively small size. Areas such as the Lower East Side can only benefit from the continuation and expansion of such activities.

13

New Programs for Group Work Agencies

Harold H. Weissman

The planners of Mobilization For Youth did not accord group services a major role in the fight against delinquency. Opportunity for work training, new educational techniques, and the organization of citizens to deal with community problems, were viewed as much more significant factors in this fight. Group-work programs were seen as the means of reaching teen-agers, of establishing relationships with them so that they could be helped to make use of the new opportunities which Mobilization would make available.

Were they correct in their assessment? The projects' results do not provide any clear answer, as in fact the agency did not put a concerted effort into group services. While there is little in the Mobilization experience to lead one to conclude that group services or group work agencies per se offer a solution to delinquency, there is some reason to believe that Mobilization, outside of its social-action organizations, did not sufficiently attempt to harness the power of peer groups to support various program ends, whether in education, work-training, or the like.

Had Mobilization, for example, formed a "union" of its work trainees, many of the problems of trainee motivation as well as ineffective practices and policies of Mobilization itself might have been more effectively dealt with. Nevertheless, a survey of its group-services programs shows that Mobilization did develop a number of program innovations. It also shows that there is a need for group-work agencies to reevaluate their relationship to other social institutions.

Program Innovations

The adolescent service center was a major innovation. These centers enabled the settlements to reach large numbers of troubled youths who not only did not come to the settlement houses but were not even reached by the detached worker programs. The visibility of the Adventure Corps through its uniforms and appearance at public events likewise recruited large numbers of previously unserved preadolescents.[1]

In addition, the Adolescent Service Centers sought out adults to help find jobs, to tutor, and to assist generally in the work of the centers. Adult involvement with individual youth was stressed as opposed to group discussion and planning. The centers operated under the premise that delinquency was not a problem which the community could hire professionals such as social workers, teachers, or psychiatrists to solve. The problem could only be solved if adults in the community involved themselves with the problem and with the adolescents who were so involved. The centers did not become the buffer or the wall behind which the adult community could hide.

The idea of involving group members in planning their activities is an old one in group work. The Young Adult Action Group experience suggests the possibility of adding to the traditional institutional offerings of clubs, gymnasiums and dancing, the opportunity to join with one's peers in social action to do something about immediate problems in one's neighborhood. Likewise the Cultural Arts Program offered a way of strengthening ethnic and racial pride.[2]

[1] The need for symbols, spectacles, and ceremonial events has not been adequately considered in social group work theory. The Adventure Corps is discussed in the chapter on "Group Service Programs and their Effect on Delinquents," Adolescent Service Centers in the chapter "Adolescent Service Centers," both in this volume.

[2] The Cultural Arts Program is discussed in the chapter on "Training Youth in the Arts," the Young Adult Action Group is discussed in the chapter "Negro Youth and Social Action," both in this volume.

Perhaps the most significant factor which emerged from the experience of the group-services programs was the need on the part of youth for a sense of competency—a sense that they can master their environment. Erikson comments about this need as follows:

> Such vindictive choices of a negative identity represent, of course, a desperate attempt at regaining some mastery in a situation in which the available positive identity elements cancel each other out. The history of such a choice reveals a set of conditions in which it is easier to derive a sense of identity out of a total identification with that which one is least supposed to be, than to struggle for a feeling of reality in acceptable roles which are unattainable . . . "At least in the gutter I'm a genius" circumscribes the relief following the total choice of a negative identity.[3]

The particular value of group-work methods in dealing with delinquencey can best be understood in the context of providing youth with a sense of competence or mastery. In a society whose major rewards go to the skilled and the educated, the slum youth who has dropped out of school and possesses no vocational skills cannot feel very competent. Traditionally group-service agencies have concerned themselves with their members' broad social competency, including inculcating values and attitudes supportive of education and work, and providing youth with sympathetic and concerned adults who could help them in their efforts to seek work or continue their education. In this vein there is another equally important function they could perform: gearing the content of certain group programs to the actual content of the school class and the work crew, thereby supporting participants in their efforts to learn and work. Mobilization experimented with one such program in the 1966–67 program year. It suggests a new emphasis for group-service agencies.

[3] Erik Erikson, "The Problem of Ego Identity," in Maurice Stein, Arthur Vidich, and David White, editors, *Identity and Anxiety* (Glencoe, Illinois, The Free Press, 1960), p. 92.

An Educationally Supportive Play Group

The Preadolescent Program, [4] designed to provide predelinquent youngsters with group activities within the confines of settlement houses, was in the main not successful in encouraging conforming activities and attitudes. Those who had engaged in delinquent activities prior to involvement in the program by and large continued in these activities. In discussing ways in which the preadolescent program might be made more effective, staff concluded that the single best indicator of predelinquency is truancy from school and general inability to function in school. Thus, it was reasoned, if a child could be helped to stay in school and to feel adequate there from the very beginning, this would have a major effect on his social attitudes and behavior outside of school.

In the fall of 1966, therefore, the Preadolescent Program became the Second Grade Program. The second grade was chosen because it was thought that by the time a child was in the third grade, his learning problems were often too far advanced for help; the first grade might be too soon to screen out the youngsters who would need and could profit from the special group program. The program deviated from traditional group-service programs in that, while it acknowledged the effect of other contexts on the child—family, peer group, neighborhood—it was specifically oriented to only one context, the classroom. Families were contacted only to gain their permission for the child's participation and to give them information about the program. The range of problems that might beset a child's family were not to be dealt with. This conception was based on the idea that while a variety of problems cause a child to become a delinquent, these problems cannot, and perhaps should not, be attacked all at once. Some have greater effect than others. The Second Grade Program was designed to determine whether school functioning is one of the more significant elements in the problem chain.

Traditionally, social group workers are trained in the use of the group as a growth and socializing experience. They are taught how to form groups, guide interaction, assess individual and group

[4] See the chapter on "Group Service Programs and Their Effects on Delinquents" in this volume for a description of this program.

development, teach problem solving and decision making. Programming is the essential tool used to accomplish these goals. The activities offered include drama, cooking, sports, games, trips, dances, etc. In the Second Grade Program, two adaptations were made in traditional group work approaches. First, the purpose of the group was not to promote the growth and development of individual members but to promote their capacity to perform the educational tasks required of them in their school class. Second, the activities of the group were designed to teach the child material related specifically to a variety of school tasks which he had to master.

In November 1966, seven settlements and churches organized one group each of underachieving second graders. Group members were recruited on the advice of teachers and school guidance personnel. Those whom the school staff judged retarded (brain injured), in need of intensive psychiatric treatment, or so handicapped that they could not participate with their peers were screened out. Each group met twice a week after school hours. In addition, each member had at least one private-tutoring session per week.

Emphasis was on maintaining the child in his class by gearing the group's programs to the educational attainments demanded of children in that class. The following excerpts from an observer's report on one of the groups illustrates this intent:

Fifth Activity—Game: Musical Chairs with Adding

How the activity was introduced: "We are going to play a game. It's like musical chairs." Chairs were set up in a line, every other chair facing the same direction. Phil established moving direction, and each child was assigned a number from one to ten. It was explained that, when the music stopped, the two children who did not get a seat would call out their numbers which the group (with the help of the group leader (would add together and then continue the game.

What was taught: Adding two numbers with a very enjoyable game. Everyone participated actively and no one was left out.

How did group respond? Very favorably. It was a familiar game, and they could add the two numbers with assistance and guessing.

How did individuals respond? They were upset that there were two chairs too few until they got into the spirit of trying to add quickly. They became more noisy and free as the game went on.

What did they learn? The experience of adding two numbers as part of a game, doing well with a familiar game. Phil was concrete in saying, "We will play two more times and then have snacks," so they knew what was coming next.

The program proved difficult to carry out for a variety of reasons. It was hard to develop the educational games and material quickly enough so that it would be available when needed to match classroom activities. The program required a reorientation of group workers' traditional approaches in that they had to develop a teaching role. Few of the workers had experience working with seven-year-olds, most of whom demanded constant individual attention. The children were extremely active, with high energy levels and short attention spans. Many of them had never owned crayons, pencils, or books of their own. Many of them did not speak English well. In order to help the workers deal with their numerous problems, weekly training sessions were instituted.

Although the children did give evidence of educational gains during the program year, it is difficult to determine the specific effects the Second Grade Program had.[5] All of the children gained in their reading levels. Yet none of the children was at the second-grade reading level at the beginning of the second grade, and none was rated at the third-grade level at the end of the second grade. One teacher rated her ten children in October at the preprimer reading level; she rated the same ten children at the end of the year at the second-grade reading level.[6] Another possible index of the

[5] For the years 1967–69, the National Institute of Mental Health assigned Mobilization a research-and-demonstration grant to carry out this program in Lower East Side schools, using experimental and control groups and a variety of other rigorous testing devices, so that the effectiveness of this programmatic innovation could be determined.

[6] One result of the first year's experience with the program is a questioning of the reliability of teacher ratings. Interviews were conducted at the end of the school year with each participating teacher. One teacher remarked, "I wanted my children to get into your program so I rated them as high as possible so you would take them." Another teacher, when confronted by the fact that children she had rated as improved in academic performance had actually been failed by her in all of their subjects, replied that she was in a particularly good mood on the day she did the final rating for the Second Grade Program.

success of the program was that attendance was extremely high, averaging well over 80 percent. In addition, every teacher requested the return of the program in the second year. There were also many examples of improved behavior and attitude as a result of participation.

Social settlements have traditionally accepted referrals from school guidance personnel of children with behavior or learning problems. These children have generally been placed in groups with a general emotional and physical growth orientation. The Second Grade Program suggests that such referrals in an urban slum area are inappropriate. First, the nature of the slum and the multiproblem family tend to dissipate gains that can be made from such group experiences. Second, the general and long-term approach of promoting growth and development does not deal with the immediate problems of the child, such as his inability to learn in school; thus it allows a situation to develop which only intensifies these problems.

Even if the Second Grade Project approach is not a viable one for underachieving children, the conception that social agencies must complement the school's attempt to educate children is worthy of further consideration. The school is clearly a much more significant institution in a child's life than a social settlement or a community center. It is also clear that children's play has a variety of purposes, and that one of them is educational. The traditional science clubs and the like in settlements are a recognition of this fact, but the connection between educational play activities in settlements and the educational needs of children in school needs to be emphasized more directly.[7]

Conclusion

Group service programs are probably best evaluated in terms of levels of goals. Although most forms of delinquency cannot be eradicated through the efforts of such programs, it is nevertheless

---

[7] This is not to say that alternate roles of settlements vis-à-vis schools should not be considered. In some cases the settlements might set themselves the task of organizing the community to change the schools. In such cases, cooperative projects such as the ones described in this paper should not be attempted, since conflicts can be anticipated.

clear that they perform valuable services.[8] Society needs links to slum youths, and slum youths, conversely, need to know adults in an informal and personal manner who can help them develop a sense of competency to function in the adult world. There is an important area of social competence which the group-service agencies have traditionally been concerned with—relationships of boy to girl, parent to child, man to man. There is also the potentiality of group service agencies programmatically supporting other institutions like the schools in their efforts to give youth a sense of competency.

It is harder for slum youths to see how they fit into society than it is for more affluent youths. Middle-class youth does not really have to concern itself with this problem until age twenty or sometimes thirty. Likewise, the more affluent can fall back on their families and the institutions of a society which are geared to their needs. When delinquency is viewed against the problem of the place and function of youth in society, then a major task for group-service agencies is clear. They must constantly press society to make available meaningful ways for youths, low-income youths in particular, to function in that society. The task is a difficult one, especially since the parents of these low-income youth, as a group and a social stratum, have themselves not yet found a secure place of their own.[9]

[8] This is not to deny that there probably would be more delinquency if such programs and their agency sponsors did not exist. Without doubt many low-income youths have been significantly affected by social agencies. Yet there are not enough such agencies, and more importantly, even if there were, their influence would not be an effective counterweight to that of the slum environment for most youth. Group work is not a solution to social problems.

[9] For a discussion of the need for a balance between youth and adult programs in settlement houses, see Harold H. Weissman and Henry Heifetz, "Changing Program Emphases of Settlement Houses," *Social Work,* Vol. 14 (October, 1968).

Index